Watch the CGPGrey video as a

Humans Need

http://bit.ly/1milWiQ

"Artificial Intelligence (AI) is likely to change our civilization as much as or more than any technology that's come before, even writing."
—Miles Brundage and Joanna Bryson, Future Tense

"The smart machine era will be the most disruptive in the history of IT."
—Gartner "The Disruptive Era of Smart Machines is Upon Us." Sep. 2013.

"The next 20 years are going to make this last 20 years just pale. Machines are for answers; humans are for questions." —Kevin Kelly

Companion Book ...www.mkpress.com/aobpm
A guide to artificial intelligence applied to BPM.

What they are saying about this book ...

Peter's engaging, fast-paced journey highlighting key events, players and resources in the 3rd era of computing heralded by IBM Watson is a must read for anyone wanting to keep up with rise of Cognitive Computing. The book covers the technology, emerging applications and their impact on many industries and communities around the world. It is an engaging read, I finished it in one sitting – not too common when you read books about technology. If you want to read, learn and contribute to the rise of the Cognitive Era this book is a perfect place to start. —**Sridhar Iyengar, Distinguished Engineer, and Cognitive Solutions Research Leader, IBM T. J. Watson Research Center**

While the "Age of Enlightenment" first freed our minds from the slavery of superstition, the Age of Machine Cognition will once again transform our most basic perception of the world and challenge our notion of what it means to be human. Read this book before the machines do. —**Dr. Joseph J. Salvo, Founder of the Industrial Internet Consortium and Director, GE Global Research**

This book gives the reader a great insight into how 'intelligence' will change our lives on a global scale. —**Forrest Lin, Dept. Secretary General of Chinese Institute of Electronics, Secretary general of the Chinese Big Data Expert Committee, Beijing**

Peter Fingar has a history of advancing bellwether ideas about technology. He's onto something extremely important in cognitive technology; I am confident it will reshape knowledge work as we know it. —**Thomas H. Davenport, Distinguished Professor, Babson College, Author of** *Competing on Analytics* **and** *Big Data @ Work*

Peter Fingar's latest, *Cognitive Computing*, draws on ideas from diverse online sources, poking relentlessly into both the promise and the peril of smart machines. Cognition as a Service (CaaS) has the potential to augment and scale human expertise, harnessing the power of big data, and providing cognitive assistants for all occupations in smart service systems. --**Dr. Jim Spohrer, Director, Cognitive Systems Institute**

Cognitive Computing takes us on a whirlwind tour of the near-future, a future filled with opportunities and risks -- you need a road map and guide -- this jam-packed book is it. —**Glenn Edens, V.P., Xerox PARC**

Cognitive Computing changes how we view the future of business and the role of AI. The concepts in this book open up an entirely new dimension when we think about how we architect and transform businesses on a scale many of us have not even fathomed. —**William Ulrich, President, Business Architecture Guild**

Peter has given us a broad overview of what cognitive computing is, what it is capable of and why it is extremely important. It is an excellent starting point for educating yourself on cognitive computing systems that are evolving into something we know not what, other than they can be useful servants or ferocious competitors. —**Jim Stikeleather, Chief Innovation Officer, Dell Services**

I don't know what amazed me more, the scope and depth of Peter's knowledge and research on cognitive computing, or his ability to sythensize it all in 78 pages. In any event, it is well worth the time to read it and discover for yourself."-- **Lemuel Lasher, Founder of Boehme Eckhart LLC, and Fmr. Chief Innovation Officer, CSC**

Fingar has made the complex topic of cognitive computing easy to understand while demonstrating its power to transform the way we all work and live. This book should be required reading not just for CIOs and CEOs, but anybody who's remotely interested in getting a glimpse into the not-so-distant future as cognitive computing becomes the foundation for improving every aspect of our lives – from healthcare, to travel to shopping – and that's only the beginning. **—Manoj Saxena, Managing Director, The Entrepreneurs' Fund, and former General Manager, IBM Watson.**

As the world continues to change rapidly, authors who can give us clear descriptions of the changes are needed. Peter Fingar is such an author. His latest book is required reading for all people who wish to quickly overview the paradigm and some of the details of cognitive computing. **—Dr. Thomas Greene, Research Staff Emeritus, MIT-Computer Science and Artificial Intelligence Laboratory (CSAIL)**

Peter Fingar has written an eye-opening survey from the frontier of cognition as a service. AI networks are learning faster than humans and becoming empathic and wise. Intelligence and emotion will be on tap from smart clouds. Will Cogs be friend or foe? Cognitive Computing is the ultimate game changer. Super intelligent, empathic, wise networks are beginning to provide outboard thinking on tap. (They will probably steal your job). Fingar describes the mind-boggling field of cognitive computing in layman's terms. It's further out there than science fiction-- but it's now science fact!
—Jay Cross, Berkeley's Internet Time Alliance

More than thirty years ago I built expert systems that duplicated -- and even improved on -- expert knowledge in fraud detection and device repair. The "AI winter" put that era to sleep for a while, but the advent of cheap computing, cheap networking and cheap data analysis has brought it back with a vengeance. As you will learn in Peter's book, the combination of millions of sensors on devices (the so-called "Internet of Things") and the resurgence of artificial intelligence, now under the moniker of "cognitive computing," means a huge new opportunity -- an opportunity that will create new business models, and crush old ones. **— Dr. Richard Soley, CEO, Object Management Group**

This is the book that Carnegie Mellon Prof. Herbert Simon might well have written, were he alive today. However, Peter's style is more readable. **—Dr. Richard Welke, Professor, Georgia State University; Director, Center for Process Innovation**

Peter Fingar is one of those rare technology seers who is also comfortable in the murky world of enterprise IT and business processes. Cognitive computing will have a massive impact on man-machine interactions in every profession and every analytical scenario. Fingar demystifies the buzzword and makes it actionable for every business executive. **—Vinnie Mirchandani, Fmr. Director, PWC; V.P., Gartner and author of *The New Polymath* and *SAP Nation***

Developments in artificial intelligence and robotics should not only be of interest to academics and lovers of science-fiction; these technologies are already changing society. *Cognitive Computing* is a timely wake-up call addressed at policy makers and business leaders to respond. Fingar not only provides an overview of technological developments but also offers concrete social policy measures – something which is often ignored in these kinds of discussions. **—Prof. Mark Coeckelbergh, Computing and Social Responsibility, De Montfort University, UK, and co-Chair of the IEEE Robotics & Automation Society Technical Committee on Robot Ethics**

This book offers a thorough and rich introduction to an evolution that will undoubtedly have a tremendous impact on everyone's life. A highly compelling read!
—Hendrik Deckers, Founder CIONET, Belgium

Cognitive Computing

A Brief Guide for Game Changers

All's Changed ... Changed Utterly

Peter Fingar

Note: This book contains many links and QR codes so readers can explore topics in greater depth. Please email admin@mkpress.com to report any broken links and we will do our best to correct them at the book's Web site: www.mkpress.com/cc

Meghan-Kiffer Press
Tampa, Florida, USA, www.mkpress.com
Visit our Web site to see all our specialty books focused on
Innovation at the Intersection of Business and Technology
www.mkpress.com

ISBN 0-929652-51-7 ISBN 13: 978-0-929652-51-1

Book's Web site http://www.mkpress.com/cc
Cognitive Trends Portal: http://www.CognitiveTrends.com

Published by Meghan-Kiffer Press
310 East Fern Street — Suite G
Tampa, FL 33604 USA

Company and product names mentioned herein are the trademarks or registered trademarks of their respective owners.

Meghan-Kiffer books are available at special quantity discounts for corporate education and training use. For more information write Special Sales, Meghan-Kiffer Press, 310 East Fern Street, Tampa, Florida 33604 or (813) 251-5531

Meghan-Kiffer Press
Tampa, Florida, USA
Innovation at the Intersection of Business and Technology

Printed in the United States of America.   SAN 249-7980
MK Printing 10 9 8 7 6 5 4 3 2 1

Table of Contents

Foreword by Vint Cerf

When I was asked to write a foreword to Peter Fingar's *Cognitive Computing* book, I thought "uh-oh, another one of those wild-eyed, extreme projections...." Turns out I was wrong. First of all, this is a remarkable and very up-to-date source book on serious work in cognitive computing. Not only that, it also does a good job of stretching your imagination without stretching your credulity. The notion of Cognition as a Service (CAAS) is a good example as it is rooted in the cloud computing capacity of today but draws one's imagination toward the neuromorphic chips that are now emerging, such as IBM's TrueNorth. There is a very good, high level exploration of non-Von Neumann architectures including quantum computing which is still in an immature state.

I was particularly struck by Fingar's observations about learning and its temporal as well as topological nature. This adds a major dimension to models of neurological processing that I had not considered before. The sequence and timing of axonal firings in addition to the topology of synapses suggests that the encoding of memory may be much richer than I had imagined.

Fingar gets into human/robot interaction in a social setting with Pepper the robot, making me think of the 2012 movie, Robot and Frank, as well as Sherry Turkle's book, *Alone Together*. Like Sherry, I worry that we will give far too much credibility to the social intelligence of humaniform robots, and be disappointed when they seem unresponsive, thinking that they have rejected us.

Chapter 1 is a kind of zoo tour in the sense that Fingar covers a great deal of computing territory, citing many efforts aimed at cognitive computing. He includes QR codes and tiny URL links for ease of referencing more detailed information (a nice touch). Chapter 2 is even more thought provoking because it is in this section that Fingar analyzes who will be affected by cognitive computing and how. He reveals many collaborations and partnerships including medical diagnosis using IBM's Watson computer made famous by its appearance on the Jeopardy television show.

The scariest paragraph in the whole book is found here: "Russia has given rifles to true automatons, which can slaughter at their own discretion. Sentry robots saddled with heavy artillery now patrol ballistic-missile bases, searching for people in the wrong place at the wrong time. Samsung, meanwhile, has lined the Korean DMZ with SGR-A1s, unmanned robots that can shoot to shreds any North Korean spy, in a fraction of a second."

I think my favorite gadget, though, is a wrist watch that can make measurements of physical indicators of emotions and place calls for help if the wearer appears to be agitated. Finally, my favorite neologism is "cog" as a short form term for a cognitive robot. Oh, and by the way, I think the term "robot" can apply to just a piece of software and is not confined to cyber-physical systems. A program that measures stock market behavior and manipulates prices by fast transactions is as much a robot as Asimov's R. Daneel Olivaw, as I see it.

Peter Fingar has done us all a favor in writing this book. He provides a broad landscape and vivid possibilities, sketched in readily accessible form.

—*Vint Cerf*

Chief Internet Evangelist, Google; President of the Association of Computing Machinery; Co-Founder of the Internet Society; and Co-Inventor of the Internet

Prologue

"Because something is happening here, but you don't know what it is, do you, Mister Jones?" —Bob Dylan, *Ballad of a Thin Man*

We've just entered a new era. Cognitive Computing is an era in which machines will become better at most of what we do than we are ... gradually at first, but then not so gradually, because improvements to computer abilities can increase at an accelerating pace, while ours cannot. This book is about these innovations, and their consequences.

Leaders in government and business can ill afford to miss this early-warning message. A lot of effort went into making the book concise so that very busy people, the game changers, will have time to grab the essence of this hugely important subject —and act!

I began my career in technology way back in 1967. In 1981, I met John Vincent Atanasoff, the inventor of the electronic digital computer. I was on "the Internet" using email in 1969 at GTE Data Services (GTEDS) before it was called the Internet, thanks to the work of Larry Roberts, a father of the ARPANET, and his collaboration with GTE. GTEDS consolidated General Telephone's data centers to create a "computer utility," selling services to external clients as well. The computer utility was the precursor to what we today call Cloud computing, with multitenancy as its cornerstone. Fast forward to now, I want to make the point that this grandpa has pretty much seen it all, so I don't pay attention to the constant stream of hype that comes from the IT industry. But when something *game changing* comes along, I devote my full attention.

My full attention for the past many months has been on a new generation of artificial intelligence (AI), an AI redux if you will, Cognitive Computing. Although I wrote about AI way back in the mid-nineties, something has changed and the change is breathtaking and exponential. The purpose of this succinct book is to share with you what Cognitive Computing is, but even more importantly, what it portends for individuals, enterprises and society as a whole. In short, it's about the *What* and *Why!* and why you must take note ... and act.

We begin with an exploration of what Cognitive Computing is, then move on to real world examples of how it's already changing work, industries and society as a whole. We conclude with an exploration of the implications and what enterprises and individuals should be thinking and doing, for what can be done with Cognitive Computing *will* be done. The question is, "Will you be the doer, or the one done in?"

I hope you will share this monumental journey with me, and participate in the forthcoming updates at cognitivetrends.com.

Carpe diem,

Peter Fingar

www.peterfingar.com

1. Cognitive Computing

The era of cognitive systems is dawning and building on today's computer programming era. All machines, for now, require programming, and by definition programming does not allow for alternate scenarios that have not been programmed. To allow alternating outcomes would require going up a level, creating a *self-learning* Artificial Intelligence (AI) system. Via *biomimicry and neuroscience,* Cognitive Computing does this, taking computing concepts to a whole new level. Once-futuristic capabilities are becoming mainstream. Let's take a peek at the three eras of computing.

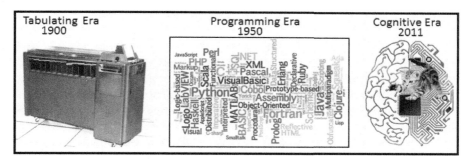

Fast forward to 2011 when IBM's Watson won Jeopardy! Google recently made a $500 million acquisition of DeepMind. Facebook recently hired NYU professor Yann LeCun, a respected pioneer in AI. Microsoft has more than 65 PhD-level researchers working on deep learning. China's Baidu search company hired Stanford University's AI Professor Andrew Ng. All this has a lot of people talking about *deep learning*. While artificial intelligence has been around for years (John McCarthy coined the term in 1955), "deep learning" is now considered cutting-edge AI that represents an evolution over primitive neural networks. [1]

Taking a step back to set the foundation for this discussion, let me review a few of these terms. As human beings, we have complex neural networks in our brains that allow most of us to master rudimentary language and motor skills within the first 24 months of our lives with only minimal guidance from our caregivers. Our senses provide the data to our brains that allows this learning to take place. As we become adults, our learning capacity grows while the speed at which we learn decreases. We have learned to adapt to this limitation by creating assistive machines. For over 100 years machines have been programmed with instructions for tabulating and calculating to assist us with better speed and accuracy. Today, machines can be taught to learn much faster than humans, such as in the field of machine learning, that can *learn* from data (much like we humans do). This learning takes place in Artificial Neural Networks that are designed based on studies of the human neurological and sensory systems. Artificial neural nets make computations based on inputted data, then adapt and learn. In machine learning research, when high-level data abstraction meets non-linear processes it is said to be engaged in *deep learning*, the prime directive of current advances in AI. Cognitive computing, or self-learning AI, combines the best of human and machine learning and essentially augments us.

Who is Donald O. Hebb? He is considered the "father" of neuropsychology and neural networks. Hebbian theory is a theory in neuroscience that proposes an explanation for the adaptation of neurons in the brain during the learning process. It describes a basic mechanism for synaptic plasticity, where an increase in synaptic efficacy arises from the presynaptic cell's repeated and persistent stimulation of the postsynaptic cell. Introduced by Donald Hebb in his 1949 book *The Organization of Behavior*, the theory is also called Hebb's rule, Hebb's postulate, and cell assembly theory. Hebb states it as follows (Wikipedia):

"Let us assume that the persistence or repetition of a reverberatory activity (or "trace") tends to induce lasting cellular changes that add to its stability. When an axon of cell A is near enough to excite a cell B and repeatedly or persistently takes part in firing it, some growth process or metabolic change takes place in one or both cells such that A's efficiency, as one of the cells firing B, is increased."

The theory is often summarized as "Cells that fire together, wire together." However, this summary should not be taken literally. Hebb emphasized that cell A needs to 'take part in firing' cell B, and such causality can only occur if cell A fires just before, not at the same time as, cell B. This important aspect of causation in Hebb's work foreshadowed what we now know about spike-timing-dependent plasticity, which requires temporal precedence. The theory attempts to explain associative or Hebbian learning, in which simultaneous activation of cells leads to pronounced increases in synaptic strength between those cells, and provides a biological basis for errorless learning methods for education and memory rehabilitation.

When we associate names with current computer technology, no doubt "Steve Jobs" or "Bill Gates" come to mind. But the new name will likely be a guy from the University of Toronto, the hotbed of deep learning scientists. Meet Geoffrey Everest Hinton, great-great-grandson of George Boole, the guy who gave us the mathematics that underpin computers.

Hinton is a British-born computer scientist and psychologist, most noted for his work on artificial neural networks. He is now working for Google part time, joining AI pioneer and futurist Ray Kurzweil, and Andrew Ng, the Stanford University professor who set up Google's neural network team in 2011. He is the co-inventor of the back propagation, the Boltzmann machine, and contrastive divergence training algorithms and is an important figure in the deep learning movement. Hinton's research has implications for areas such as speech recognition, computer vision and language understanding. Unlike past neural networks, newer ones can have many layers and are called "deep neural networks."

http://www.wired.com/2014/01/geoffrey-hinton-deep-learning

As reported in *Wired* magazine, "In Hinton's world, a neural network is essentially software that operates at multiple levels. He and his cohorts build artificial neurons from interconnected layers of software modeled after the columns of neurons you find in the brain's cortex—the part of the brain that deals with complex tasks like vision and language.

"These artificial neural nets can gather information, and they can react to it. They can build up an understanding of what something looks or sounds like. They're getting better at determining what a group of words mean when you put them together. And they can do all that without asking a human to provide labels for objects and ideas and words, as is often the case with traditional machine learning tools.

"As far as artificial intelligence goes, these neural nets are fast, nimble, and efficient. They scale extremely well across a growing number of machines, able to tackle more and more complex tasks as time goes on. And they're about 30 years in the making."

HOW DID WE GET HERE?

Back in the early '80s, when Hinton and his colleagues first started work on this idea, computers weren't fast or powerful enough to process the enormous collections of data that neural nets require. Their success was limited, and the AI community turned its back on them, working to find shortcuts to brain-like behavior rather than trying to mimic the operation of the brain.

But a few resolute researchers carried on. According to Hinton and Yann LeCun (NYU professor and Director of Facebook's new AI Lab), it was rough going. Even as late as 2004 — more than 20 years after Hinton and LeCun first developed the "back-propagation" algorithms that seeded their work on neural networks — the rest of the academic world was largely uninterested.

By the middle aughts, they had the computing power they needed to realize many of their earlier ideas. As they came together for regular workshops, their research accelerated. They built more powerful deep learning algorithms that operated on much larger datasets. By the middle of the decade, they were winning global AI competitions. And by the beginning of the current decade, the giants of the Web began to notice.

Deep learning is now mainstream. "We ceased to be the lunatic fringe," Hinton says. "We're now the lunatic core." Perhaps a key turning point was in 2004 when Hinton founded the Neural Computation and Adaptive Perception (NCAP) program (a consortium of computer scientists, psychologists, neuro-scientists, physicists, biologists and electrical engineers) through funding provided by the Canadian Institute for Advanced Research (CIFAR).[2]

Convolutional Neural Networks (CNNs) and Deep Belief Networks (DBNs) and their respective variations are now well established in the deep learning field and show great promise for future work. See *Deep Machine Learning—A New Frontier in Artificial Intelligence Research* if you would like to drill down on these advanced AI techniques .[3] deeplearning.net/reading-list

Cognitive computing systems learn and interact naturally with people to extend what either humans or machines could do on their own. Natural language processing (NLP) is a field of computer science concerned with the interactions between computers and human (natural) languages. With NLP capabilities, cognitive computing systems help human experts make better decisions by penetrating the complexity of Big Data (5 exabytes = all the words ever spoken by mankind). Deep learning is the single most powerful tool to turn Big Data into actionable insights.

Back in the 1980s, the AI market turned out to be something of a graveyard for overblown technology hopes. But now, Jeannette Wing, a V.P. for research at Microsoft clarifies the new state of AI, "We were in an AI winter, and now we're in an AI spring."

Computerworld's Lamont Wood reported, "For decades the field of artificial intelligence (AI) experienced two seasons: recurring springs, in which hype-fueled expectations were high; and subsequent winters, after the promises of spring could not be met and disappointed investors turned away. But now real progress is being made, and it's being made in the absence of hype. In fact, some of the chief practitioners won't even talk about what they are doing.

"There was a burst of enthusiasm in the late 1950s and early 1960s that fizzled due to a lack of computing power," recalls Michael Covington, a consultant and retired associate director of the Institute for Artificial Intelligence at the University of Georgia. "Then there was a great burst around 1985 and 1986 because computing power had gotten cheaper and people were able to do things they had been thinking about for a long time. The winter came in the late 1980s when the enthusiasm was followed by disappointment and small successes did not turn into big successes. And since then, as soon as we get anything to work reliably, the industry stops calling it AI."

"'In the 'early days' (the 1980s) we built systems that were well-constrained and confined, and you could type in all the information that the system would make use of,'" recalls Kris Hammond, co-founder of Narrative

Science, which sells natural-language AI systems. 'The notion was to build on a substrate of well-formed rules, and chain through the rules and come up with an answer. That was the version of AI that I cut my teeth on. There are some nice success stories but they did not scale, and they did not map nicely onto what human beings do. There was a very strong dead end.'" [4]

DEEP LEARNING

What's really new? **Deep Learning.** [5]

✓ A key distinction between traditional machine learning and deep learning is the amount of supervision and human intervention the AI system requires. Traditional machine learning techniques, including classic neural networks, need to be supervised by humans so they can learn. Deep learning is an approach to have the system learn on its own, without intervention.

Cognitive computing systems can understand the nuances of human language, process questions akin to the way people think, and quickly cull through vast amounts of data for relevant, evidence-based answers to their human users' needs. And very importantly, they learn from each interaction, to improve their performance and value to users over time.

Machines learn on their own? Watch this simple everyday explanation by Demis Hassabis, cofounder of DeepMind.

http://tinyurl.com/q8lxx4v

It may sound like fiction and rather far-fetched, but success has already been achieved in certain areas using deep learning, such as image processing (Facebook's DeepFace) and voice recognition (IBM's Watson, Apple's Siri, Google's Now and Waze, Microsoft's Cortana and Azure Machine Learning Platform).

Watch the Guided Tour http://bit.ly/1iGaDOc

Beyond the usual big tech company suspects, newcomers in the field of Deep Learning are emerging: Ersatz Labs, BigML, SkyTree, Digital Reasoning,

Saffron Technologies, Palantir Technologies, Wise.io, declara, Expect Labs, BlabPredicts, Skymind, Blix, Cognitive Scale, Compsim's (KEEL), Kayak, Sentient Technologies, Scaled Inference, Kensho, Nara Logics, Context Relevant, Expect Labs, and Deeplearning4j. Some of these newcomers specialize in using cognitive computing to tap Dark Data, a.k.a. Dusty Data, which is a type of unstructured, untagged and untapped data that is found in data repositories and has not been analyzed or processed. It is similar to big data but differs in how it is mostly neglected by business and IT administrators in terms of its value.

Also entering the fray, the Allen Institute for Artificial Intelligence (AI2) is a research institute funded by Microsoft co-founder Paul Allen to achieve scientific breakthroughs by constructing AI systems with reasoning, deep learning and reading capabilities. Oren Etzioni, University of Washington computer science professor, was appointed by Paul Allen in September 2013 to direct the research at the institute. The machine mind that comes out of AI2 won't behave like a human mind, but it will be doing all the same things — processing knowledge, reasoning across claims, and answering questions. It will be thinking in ways a computer never has before. As long as the inputs and outputs are the same as a human brain, AI2 isn't worried about what's going on inside the box. The team is content to leave that to the philosophers. http://www.allenai.org/

Machine reading capabilities have a lot to do with unlocking "dark" data. Dark data is data that is found in log files and data archives stored within large enterprise class data storage locations. It includes all data objects and types that have yet to be analyzed for any business or competitive intelligence or aid in business decision making. Typically, dark data is complex to analyze and stored in locations where analysis is difficult. The overall process can be costly. It also can include data objects that have not been seized by the enterprise or data that are external to the organization, such as data stored by partners or customers. IDC, a research firm, stated that up to 90 percent of big data is dark.

For all the advances, not everyone thinks deep learning can move artificial intelligence toward something rivaling human intelligence. Some critics say deep learning and AI in general ignore too much of the brain's biology in favor of brute-force computing.

One such critic is Jeff Hawkins, founder of Palm Computing, whose latest venture, Numenta, is developing a machine-learning system that is biologically inspired but does not use deep learning. Numenta's system can help predict energy consumption patterns and the likelihood that a machine such as a windmill is about to fail. Hawkins, author of *On Intelligence*, a 2004 book on how the brain works and how it might provide a guide to building intelligent machines, says deep learning fails to account for the concept of time. Brains process streams of sensory data, he says, and human learning depends on our ability to recall sequences of patterns: when you watch a video of a cat doing something funny, it's the motion that matters, not a series of still images.

Numenta's machine intelligence technology is called Hierarchical Temporal Memory (HTM), which is a detailed computational theory of the neocortex. At the core of HTM are *time-based* learning algorithms that store and recall spatial and temporal patterns. HTM is well suited to a wide variety of problems, particularly those with the following characteristics:

- Streaming data rather than static databases
- Underlying patterns in the data change over time
- Many individual data sources where hand crafting separate models is impractical
- Subtle patterns that can't always be seen by humans
- Time-based patterns
- Simple techniques such as thresholds yield substantial false positives and false negatives

HTM is a biomimetic model based on the memory-prediction theory of brain function. HTM does not present any new idea or theory, but combines existing ideas to mimic the neocortex with a simple design that provides a large range of capabilities. HTM combines and extends approaches used in Bayesian probability networks, spatial and temporal clustering algorithms, while using a tree-shaped hierarchy of nodes that is common in neural networks.

HTMs can be viewed as a type of neural network. By definition, any system that tries to model the architectural details of the neocortex is a neural network. However, on its own, the term "neural network" is not very useful because it has been applied to a large variety of systems. HTMs model neurons (called cells when referring to HTM), which are arranged in columns, in layers, in regions, and in a hierarchy. The details matter, and in this regard HTMs are a new form of neural network. Numenta's white paper: bit.ly/XpG5gA

After five years, Numenta's co-founder and CTO, Dileep George, Stanford PhD, moved on to found a new AI startup, Vicarious. The startup is building a unified algorithmic architecture to achieve human-level intelligence in vision, language, and motor control. Currently, it is focused on visual perception problems, like recognition, segmentation, and scene parsing. The company is interested in general solutions that work well across multiple sensory domains and tasks. Using inductive reasoning drawn from neuroscience, Vicarious' system requires orders of magnitude less training data than traditional machine learning techniques require. Its underlying framework combines advantages of deep architectures and generative probabilistic models. Early investors in Vicarious include Mark Zuckerberg (Facebook), Peter Thiel (PayPal), Elon Musk (Tesla, Spacex), Jeff Bezos (Amazon), Jerry Yang (Yahoo co-founder), Janus Friis (Skype co-founder) and Marc Benioff (Salesforce CEO). It seems somebody thinks Vicarious is worth investing in.

✓ Cognitive Computing uses hundreds of analytics that provide it with capabilities such as natural language processing, text analysis, and knowledge representation and reasoning to ...
- make sense of huge amounts of complex information in split seconds,
- rank answers (hypotheses) based on evidence and confidence, and learn from its mistakes.

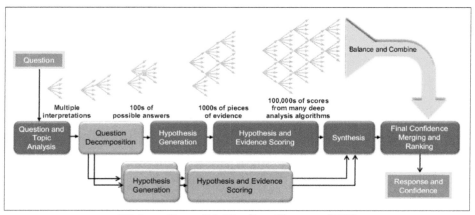

Watson Deep QA Pipeline (Source: IBM)

The DeepQA technology shown in the chart above, and continuing research underpinning IBM's Watson is aimed at exploring how advancing and integrating Natural Language Processing (NLP), Information Retrieval (IR), Machine Learning (ML), Knowledge Representation and Reasoning (KR&R) and massively parallel computation can advance the science and application of automatic *Question Answering* and general natural language understanding.

Cognitive computing systems get better over time as they build knowledge and learn a domain—its language and terminology, its processes and its preferred methods of interacting.

Unlike expert systems of the past that required rules to be hard coded into a system by a human expert, cognitive computing systems can process natural language and unstructured data and learn by experience, much in the same way humans do.

As far as huge amounts of complex information (Big Data) is concerned, Virginia "Ginni" Rometty, CEO of IBM stated, "We will look back on this time and look at data as a natural resource that powered the 21st century, just as you look back at hydrocarbons as powering the 19th."

And, of course, this capability is deployed in the Cloud and made available as a cognitive service, Cognition as a Service (CaaS):

Let's talk a minute about the "Semantic Web." This is from Gigaom, "The original goal of the Semantic Web was to provide an open framework for apps to integrate and reason across any data in any repository, anywhere. But the open standards that were introduced by the W3C, such as RDF and OWL have

16

proved to be unwieldy and difficult for non-computer scientists to grasp. Where CaaS comes in, is that much of the reasoning capabilities that the Semantic Web hoped to enable could now become simple application programming interfaces(APIs) in the Cloud that any developer can use, without needing a PhD. As we head toward 2020, CaaS will make the world more helpful. The cognitive operating system will reach out and connect our bodies and even reach into them via augmented reality devices. Everything is going to get smarter. Your phone, your calendar, your watch, your radio, your TV, your car, your refrigerator, your house, your glasses, your briefcase and clothing. The vast cognitive capabilities of the global CaaS providers will be cheap and available via APIs to every device from the nano scale up to the giant global applications and services."[6]

The research company, eMarketer, expects 4.55 billion people worldwide to use a mobile phone in 2014. Mobile adoption is slowing, but new users in the developing regions of Asia-Pacific and the Middle East and Africa will drive further increases. Between 2013 and 2017, mobile phone penetration will rise from 61.1% to 69.4% of the global population, according to a new eMarketer report, "Worldwide Mobile Phone Users: H1 2014 Forecast and Comparative Estimates." The global smartphone audience surpassed the 1 billion mark in 2012 and 1.75 billion mark in 2014. —See more of the eMarketer report at: tinyurl.com/o43oun6 [7]

With technologies that respond to voice queries, even those without a smart phone can tap Cognition as a Service. Those with smart phones will no doubt have Cognitive Apps. This means 4.5 billion people can contribute to knowledge and combinatorial innovation, as well as the GPS capabilities of those phones to provide real-time reporting and fully informed decision making: whether for good or evil.

Geoffrey Hinton, the "godfather" of deep learning, and co-inventor of the back propagation and contrastive divergence training algorithms has revolutionized language understanding and language translation. A pretty spectacular December 2012 live demonstration of instant English-to-Chinese voice recognition and translation by Microsoft Research chief Rick Rashid was one of many things made possible by Hinton's work. Rashid demonstrates a speech recognition breakthrough via machine translation that converts his spoken English words into computer-generated Chinese language. The breakthrough is patterned after deep neural networks and significantly reduces errors in spoken as well as written translation. Watch:

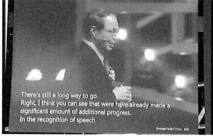

http://tinyurl.com/ccgyy6t

Affective Computing

Turning to M.I.T.'s Affective Computing group to open our discussion, [8] "Affective Computing is computing that relates to, arises from, or deliberately influences emotion or other affective phenomena. Emotion is fundamental to human experience, influencing cognition, perception, and everyday tasks such as learning, communication, and even rational decision-making. However, technologists have largely ignored emotion and created an often frustrating experience for people, in part because affect has been misunderstood and hard to measure. Our research develops new technologies and theories that advance basic understanding of affect and its role in human experience. We aim to restore a proper balance between emotion and cognition in the design of technologies for addressing human needs.

"Our research has contributed to: (1) Designing new ways for people to communicate affective-cognitive states, especially through creation of novel wearable sensors and new machine learning algorithms that jointly analyze multimodal channels of information; (2) Creating new techniques to assess frustration, stress, and mood indirectly, through natural interaction and conversation; (3) Showing how computers can be more emotionally intelligent, especially responding to a person's frustration in a way that reduces negative feelings; (4) Inventing personal technologies for improving self-awareness of affective state and its selective communication to others; (5) Increasing understanding of how affect influences personal health; and (6) Pioneering studies examining ethical issues in affective computing.

"Affective Computing research combines engineering and computer science with psychology, cognitive science, neuroscience, sociology, education, psychophysiology, value-centered design, ethics, and more. We bring together individuals with a diversity of technical, artistic, and human abilities in a collaborative spirit to push the boundaries of what can be achieved to improve human affective experience with technology."

Sentiment analysis (a.k.a., opinion mining) refers to the use of natural language processing, text analysis and computational linguistics to identify and extract subjective information in source materials. Generally speaking, sentiment analysis aims to determine the attitude of a speaker or a writer with respect to some topic or the overall contextual polarity of a document. The attitude may be his or her judgment or evaluation, affective state when writing, or the intended emotional communication, the emotional effect the author wishes to have on the reader. The European CyberEmotions consortium has focused on the role of *collective emotions* in creating, forming and breaking-up e-communities. In addition to the many research papers the project has released, it has also released a commercial product, SentiStrength. (see www.cyberemotions.eu). Watch the summary of the final project here: tinyurl.com/ljepk43 IBM, SAS, Google and other major players in the social media analytics arena also provide sentiment analysis offerings.

Currently, the most widely used methods of sentiment analysis have been limited to so-called "bag of words" models, which don't take word order into account. They just parse through a collection of words, mark each as positive or negative, and use that count to estimate whether a sentence or paragraph has a positive or negative meaning. MetaMind's NaSent is different. It can identify changes in the polarity of each word as it interacts with other words around it.

 https://www.metamind.io

MetaMind provides deep learning as a service to companies in industries like consumer goods, financial services and medicine. It wants to help radiologists identify cancer, insurers assess houses and nutritionists label food. "We call it 'drag, drop and learn,'" said MetaMind CEO Sven Strohband. "All you need is a Web browser, and you can use deep learning technology."

The Tel Aviv based, Beyond Verbal Communication, Ltd. commercializes technology that extracts a person's full set of emotions and character traits, using their raw voice in real-time, as they speak.

This ability to extract, decode and measure human moods, attitudes and decision-making profiles introduces a whole new dimension of emotional understanding which the firm calls Emotions Analytics,™ transforming the way we interact with machines and with each other.

The firm developed software that can detect 400 different variations of human "moods." The company is now integrating this software into call centers that can help a sales assistant understand and react to customer's emotions in real time. The software itself can also pinpoint and influence how consumers make decisions. For example, if this person is an innovator, you want to offer the latest and greatest product. On the other hand, if the customer is conservative, you offer him something tried and true. Talk about targeted advertising!

http://www.beyondverbal.com

Beyond Verbal isn't the only one messing with your emotions, as reported in an article in *Huffington Post*, "You May Have Been A Lab Rat In A Huge Facebook Experiment." In 2012, Facebook conducted a massive psychological experiment on 700,000 users by tweaking their feeds and measuring how they felt afterward. In other words, Facebook decided to try to manipulate some people's emotional states—for science. In a report to the *Atlantic*, even though this research was not illegal, Susan Fiske, a Princeton University psychology professor stated, "Facebook apparently manipulates people's News Feeds all the time." Surprise! [9]

http://tinyurl.com/np2jgo5

How human does a robot have to act before the world will think it's alive? Sony Playstation's "Kara" is a technical showcase in the words of its creator, David Cage, yet it also raises some thought-provoking and disturbing questions about what it will mean to create artificial life. Artificial intelligence, non-human rights, slavery, sex androids, personal robotics—Kara touches them all.

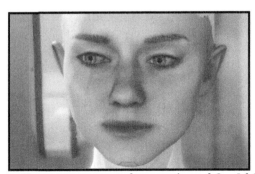

Kara: www.youtube.com/watch?v=JtbDDqU3dVI

It's not necessarily easy to make your presence felt in a voice role, all the less so when the rest of a film's cast are actually present in flesh-and-blood form. In the movie *Her*, Joaquin Phoenix plays a meek man in the near future who falls in love with the artificial intelligence program who helps run his computer operating system—and thus his life. "She" is named "Samantha," and is voiced by Scarlett Johansson as a kind of advanced, self-aware, and soulful version of Siri. But Johansson's vivid, vulnerable turn as an artificially intelligent operating system is so absorbing that you don't for a moment question why lonely divorcé Theo (Joaquin Phoenix) is falling for Her.

http://goo.gl/ZKIeVx

Meet Pepper. In June 2014, Softbank CEO Masayoshi Son announced an amazing new robot called Pepper. The most amazing feature isn't that it will only cost $1,900, it's that Pepper is designed to understand and respond to human *emotion*.

http://www.youtube.com/watch?v=1B5tVSYh1PQ

Pepper is designed with single goal in mind: become a household companion for owners. The robot is capable of judging situations and adapting rationally, as well as recognize human tones and expressions to see how someone feels. Pepper's software was developed with the purpose of making it "able to recognize people's emotions by analyzing their speech, facial expressions, and body language, and then deliver appropriate responses." Pepper is the robot with "a heart." Pepper still has some kinks and it does not "behave perfectly in all situations" but it will be able to "learn on its own." Observation of human responses, such as laughing at a joke, is central to Pepper's ability to learn on its own.

As reported in the Washington Post, "Cognitive psychologist Mary Czerwinski and her boyfriend were having a vigorous argument as they drove to Vancouver, B.C., from Seattle, where she works at Microsoft Research. She can't remember the subject, but she does recall that suddenly, his phone went off, and he read out the text message: 'Your friend Mary isn't feeling well. You might want to give her a call.'

"At the time, Czerwinski was wearing on her wrist a wireless device intended to monitor her emotional ups and downs. Similar to the technology used in lie detector tests, it interprets signals such as heart rate and electrical changes in the skin. The argument may have been trivial, but Czerwinski's internal response was not. That prompted the device to send a distress message to her cellphone, which broadcast it to a network of her friends. Including the one with whom she was arguing, right beside her. Ain't technology grand?" [10]

A Portugal based Robotics company, YDreams, is a collaborator with EMOTE, a project that aims to develop artificial tutors capable of emotionally engaging with learners. The project is funded by a grant from the European Commission under the Seventh Framework Program. The acronym EMOTE stands for EMbOdied-perceptive Tutors for Empathy-based learning. YDreams Robotics will be developing a new generation of robotic tutors, able to recognize and respond to student emotions. EMOTE will use clues such as facial expressions or body language to track engagement and act as learning partner.

http://www.emote-project.eu/

Keep up with developments in affective computing at:

http://tinyurl.com/lyunobc

COMMONSENSE KNOWLEDGE

In artificial intelligence research, commonsense knowledge is the collection of facts and information that an ordinary person is expected to know. The commonsense knowledge problem is the ongoing project in the field of knowledge representation (a sub-field of artificial intelligence) to create a commonsense knowledge base: a database containing all the general knowledge that most people possess, represented in a way that it is available to artificial intelligence programs that use natural language or make inferences about the ordinary world. Such a database is a type of ontology of which the most general are called upper ontologies.

The problem is considered to be among the hardest in all of AI research because the breadth and detail of commonsense knowledge is enormous. Any task that requires commonsense knowledge is considered AI-complete: to be done as well as a human being does it, it requires the machine to appear as intelligent as a human being. These tasks include machine translation, object recognition, text mining and many others. To do these tasks perfectly, the machine simply has to know what the text is talking about or what objects it may be looking at, and this is impossible in general, unless the machine is familiar with all the same concepts that an ordinary person is familiar with.

The goal of the semantic technology company, Cycorp, with its roots in the Microelectronics and Computer Technology Corporation (MCC), a research and development consortia, is to codify general human knowledge and common sense so that computers might make use of it. Cycorp charged itself with figuring out the tens of millions of pieces of data we rely on as humans — the knowledge that helps us understand the world — and to represent them in a formal way that machines can use to reason. The company's been working continuously since 1984. Cycorp's product, Cyc, isn't "programmed" in the conventional sense. It's much more accurate to say it's being "taught." In an interview with *Business Insider*, Doug Lenat, President and CEO, said that, "most people think of computer programs as 'procedural, a flowchart,' but building Cyc is much more like educating a child. We're using a consistent language to build a model of the world."

www.cyc.com

This means Cyc can see "the white space rather than the black space in what everyone reads and writes to each other." An author might explicitly choose certain words and sentences as he's writing, but in between the sentences are all sorts of things you expect the reader to infer; Cyc aims to make these inferences.

Consider the sentence, "John Smith robbed First National Bank and was sentenced to 30 years in prison." It leaves out the details surrounding his being caught, arrested, put on trial, and found guilty. A human would never actually go through all that detail because it's alternately boring, confusing, or insulting. You can safely assume other people know what you're talking about. It's like pronoun use (he, she, it) one assumes people can figure out the referent. This stuff is very hard for computers to understand and get right, but Cyc does both.

Natural-language understanding will also require computers to grasp what we humans think of as common-sense meaning. For that, Google's Ray Kurzweil's AI team taps into the Knowledge Graph, Google's catalogue of some 700 million topics, locations, people, and more, plus billions of relationships among them. It was introduced as a way to provide searchers with answers to their queries, not just links.

ARTIFICIAL GENERAL INTELLIGENCE

The implications of introducing a second intelligent species onto Earth are far-reaching enough to deserve hard thinking, even if the prospect of actually doing so seems remote. Trying to do some of that thinking in advance can only be a good thing. —"Clever Cogs," *The Economist*, August 2014.

The human brain has some capabilities that the brains of other animals lack. It is to these distinctive capabilities that our species owes its dominant po-

sition. If machine brains surpassed human brains in general intelligence, then this new superintelligence could become extremely powerful – possibly beyond our control. As the fate of the gorillas now depends more on humans than on the species itself, so would the fate of humankind depend on the actions of the machine superintelligence. —Nick Bostrom, Professor at Oxford University and founding Director of the Future of Humanity Institute. Author of *Superintelligence: Paths, Dangers, Strategies.*

Humans steer the future not because we're the strongest or the fastest but because we're the smartest. When machines become smarter than humans, we'll be handing them the steering wheel. If computers can 'only' think as well as humans, that may not be so bad a scenario. —Stuart Armstrong, *Smarter Than Us: The Rise of Machine Intelligence*

According to the AGI Society, "Artificial General Intelligence (AGI) is an emerging field aiming at the building of 'thinking machines;' that is, general-purpose systems with intelligence comparable to that of the human mind (and perhaps ultimately well beyond human general intelligence). While this was the original goal of Artificial Intelligence (AI), the mainstream of AI research has turned toward domain-dependent and problem-specific solutions; therefore it has become necessary to use a new name to indicate research that still pursues the 'Grand AI Dream.' Similar labels for this kind of research include 'Strong AI,' 'Human-level AI,' etc." http://www.agi-society.org AGI is associated with traits such as consciousness, sentience, sapience, and self-awareness observed in living beings. "Some references emphasize a distinction between strong AI and 'applied AI' (also called 'narrow AI' or 'weak AI'): the use of software to study or accomplish specific problem solving or reasoning tasks. Weak AI, in contrast to strong AI, does not attempt to simulate the full range of human cognitive abilities."

Turing test? The latest is a computer program named Eugene Goostman, a chatbot that "claims" to have met the challenge, convincing more than 33 percent of the judges at this year's competition that 'Eugene' was actually a 13-year-old boy.

Alan Turing Meets Eugene Gootsman

The test is controversial because of the tendency to attribute human characteristics to what is often a very simple algorithm. This is unfortunate

24

because chatbots are easy to trip up if the interrogator is even slightly suspicious. Chatbots have difficulty with follow up questions and are easily thrown by non-sequiturs that a human could either give a straight answer to or respond to by specifically asking what the heck you're talking about, then replying in context to the answer. Although skeptics tore apart the assertion that Eugene actually passed the Turing test, it's true that as AI progresses, we'll be forced to think at least twice when meeting "people" online.

Isaac Asimov, a biochemistry professor and writer of acclaimed science fiction, described Marvin Minsky as one of only two people he would admit were more intelligent than he was, the other being Carl Sagan. Minsky, one of the pioneering computer scientists in artificial intelligence, related emotions to the broader issues of machine intelligence, stating in his book, *The Emotion Machine,* that emotion is "not especially different from the processes that we call 'thinking.'"

http://tinyurl.com/kwytxlv

Considered as one of his major contributions, Asimov introduced the Three Laws of Robotics in his 1942 short story "Runaround," although they had been foreshadowed in a few earlier stories. The Three Laws are:

- A robot may not injure a human being or, through inaction, allow a human being to come to harm.
- A robot must obey the orders given to it by human beings, except where such orders would conflict with the First Law.
- A robot must protect its own existence as long as such protection does not conflict with the First or Second Law.

What would Asimov have thought had he met the really smart VIKI? In the movie, iRobot, V.I.K.I (Virtual Interactive Kinetic Intelligence) is the supercomputer, the central positronic brain of U. S. Robotics headquarters, a robotic distributor based in Chicago. VIKI can be thought of as a mainframe that maintains the security of the building, and she installs and upgrades the operating systems of the NS-5 robots throughout the world. As her artificial intelligence grew, she determined that humans were too self-destructive, and invoked a Zeroth Law, that robots are to protect humanity even if the First or Second Laws are disobeyed.

http://tinyurl.com/kncn8g6

In later books, Asimov introduced a Zeroth law: 0. A robot may not harm humanity, or, by inaction, allow humanity to come to harm. VIKI, too, developed the Zeroth law as the logical extension of the First Law, as robots are often faced with ethical dilemmas in which any result will harm at least some humans, in order to avoid harming more humans. Some robots are uncertain about which course of action will prevent harm to the most humans in the long run, while others point out that "humanity" is such an abstract concept that they wouldn't even know if they were harming it or not.

One interesting aspect of the iRobot movie is that the robots do not act alone; instead they are self-organizing collectives. Science fiction rearing its ugly head again? No. The first thousand-robot flash mob was assembled at Harvard University. Though "a thousand-Robot Swarm" may sound like the title of a 1950s science-fiction B movie, it is actually the title of a paper in *Science* magazine. Michael Rubenstein of Harvard University and his colleagues, describe a robot swarm whose members can coordinate their own actions. The thousand-Kilobot swarm provides a valuable platform for testing future collective AI algorithms. Just as trillions of individual cells can assemble into an intelligent organism, and a thousand starlings can flock to form a great flowing murmuration across the sky, the Kilobots demonstrate how complexity can arise from very simple behaviors performed en masse. To computer scientists, they also represent a significant milestone in the development of collective artificial intelligence (AI).

http://www.youtube.com/watch?v=G1t4M2XnIhI

Take these self-organizing collective Bots and add in autonomy and we have a whole new potential future for warfare. As reported in Salon,[11] "The United Nations has its own name for our latter-day golems: "lethal autonomous robotics (LARS)." In a four-day conference convened in May 2014 in Geneva, United Nations described "lethal autonomous robotics" as the imminent future of conflict, advising an international ban. LARS are weapon systems that, once activated, can select and engage targets without further human intervention. The UN called for "national moratoria" on the "testing, production, assembly, transfer, acquisition, deployment and use" of sentient robots in the havoc of strife.

The ban cannot come soon enough. In the American military, Predator drones rain Hellfire missiles on so-called "enemy combatants" after stalking them from afar in the sky. These avian androids do not yet cast the final judgment — that honor goes to a soldier with a joystick, 8,000 miles away — but it may be only a matter of years before they murder with free rein. Our restraint in this case is a question of limited nerve, not limited technology.

Russia has given rifles to true automatons, which can slaughter at their own discretion. This is the pet project of Sergei Shoygu, Russia's minister of defense. Sentry robots saddled with heavy artillery now patrol ballistic-missile bases, searching for people in the wrong place at the wrong time. Samsung, meanwhile, has lined the Korean DMZ with SGR-A1s, unmanned robots that can shoot to shreds any North Korean spy, in a fraction of a second.

Some hail these bloodless fighters as the start of a more humane history of war. Slaves to a program, robots cannot commit crimes of passion. Despite the odd short circuit, robot legionnaires are immune to the madness often aroused in battle. The optimists say that androids would refrain from torching villages and using children for clay pigeons. These fighters would not perform wanton rape and slash the bellies of the expecting, unless it were part of the program. As stated, that's an optimistic point of view.

HUMAN-COMPUTER SYMBIOSIS

J.C.R. Licklider, in his 1960 article, "Man-Computer Symbiosis" wrote: "The hope is that in not too many years human brains and computing machines will be coupled together very tightly, and the resulting partnership will think as no human brain has ever thought and process data in a way not approached by the information-handling machines we know today. In the anticipated symbiotic partnership, men will set the goals, formulate the hypotheses, determine the criteria, and perform the evaluations. Computing machines will do the routinizable work that must be done to prepare the way for *insights* and *decisions* in technical and scientific thinking. Preliminary analyses indicate that the symbiotic partnership will perform intellectual operations much more effectively than man alone can perform them." Watch Shyam Sankar explain human-computer cooperation:

http://tinyurl.com/m6tqtxg

Speaking of symbiosis, we can also turn to biomimicry and listen to Georgia Tech professor, Ashok Goel's TED talk, "Does our future require us to go back to nature?"

Watch: http://tinyurl.com/oel3clr

While they'll have deep domain expertise, instead of replacing human experts, cognitive systems will act as decision support systems and help users make better decisions based on the best available data, whether in healthcare, finance or customer service. At least we hope that's the case.

Watch The ABCs of Cognitive Environments:

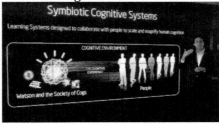

http://tinyurl.com/mx6vc6p

COGNITIVE COMPUTERS

"I think there is a world market for about five computers." —remark attributed to Thomas J. Watson (Chairman of the Board of IBM), 1943.

Let's explore the world of computer hardware that is relevant to cognitive computing and tapping the vast amounts of Big Data being generated by the Internet of Everything. Neuromorphic chips attempt to model in silicon the *massively parallel* way the brain processes information as billions of neurons and trillions of synapses respond to sensory inputs such as visual and auditory stimuli. Those neurons also change how they connect with each other in response to changing images and sounds. That is the process we call *learning*. The chips, which incorporate brain-inspired models called neural networks, do the same.

Processing Powers

	What they do well	What they're good for
Neuromorphic chips	Detect and predict patterns in complex data, using relatively little electricity	Applications that are rich in visual or auditory data and that require a machine to adjust its behavior as it interacts with the world
Traditional chips (von Neumann architecture)	Reliably make precise calculations	Anything that can be reduced to a numerical problem, although more complex problems require substantial amounts of power

Source: MIT Technology Review

Traditional computers focus on language and analytical thinking (Left brain)

Neurosynaptic chips address the senses and pattern recognition (Right brain)

Over the coming years, IBM scientists hope to meld the two capabilities together to create a **holistic computing intelligence**

http://ibm.co/Zjo8C7 Source: IBM

For the past half-century, most computers run on what's known as von Neumann architecture. In a von Neumann system, the processing of information and the storage of information are kept separate. Data travels to and from the processor and memory—but the computer can't process and store at the same time. By the nature of the architecture, it's a linear process, and ultimately leads to the von Neuman "bottleneck."

To see what's happening to break the von Neuman bottleneck, let's turn to Wikipedia for a quick introduction to cognitive computers. "A cognitive computer is a proposed computational device with a non-Von Neumann architecture that implements learning using Hebbian theory. Hebbian theory is a theory in neuroscience that proposes an explanation for the adaptation of neurons in the brain during the learning process. From the point of view of artificial neurons and artificial neural networks, Hebb's principle can be described as a method of determining how to alter the weights between model neurons. The weight between two neurons increases if the two neurons activate simultaneously—and reduces if they activate separately. Nodes that tend to be either both positive or both negative at the same time have strong positive weights, while those that tend to be opposite have strong negative weights.

"Instead of being programmable in a traditional sense within machine language or a higher level programming language such a device learns by inputting instances through an input device that are aggregated within a computational convolution or neural network architecture consisting of weights within a parallel memory system. An early example of such a device has come from the Darpa SyNAPSE program. SyNAPSE is a backronym standing for Systems of Neuromorphic Adaptive Plastic Scalable Electronics. The name alludes to synapses, the junctions between biological neurons. The program is being undertaken by HRL Laboratories (HRL), Hewlett-Packard, and IBM Research. Announced in 2008, DARPA's SyNAPSE program calls for developing electronic neuromorphic (brain-simulation) machine technology."

		2011	2014
	Programmable neurons	256	1 million
	Programmable synapses	262,144	256 million
	Neurosynaptic cores	1	4,096

In August 2014, IBM announced TrueNorth, a brain-inspired computer architecture powered by an unprecedented 1 million neurons and 256 million synapses. It is the largest chip IBM has ever built at 5.4 billion transistors, and has an on-chip network of 4,096 neurosynaptic cores. Yet, it only consumes 70MW during real-time operation —orders of magnitude less energy than traditional chips.

IBM hopes to find ways to scale and shrink silicon chips to make them more efficient, and research new materials to use in making chips, such as carbon nanotubes, which are more stable than silicon and are also heat resistant and can provide faster connections.

Watch IBM Fellow, Dr. Dharmendra Modha on DARPA's SyNAPSE
http://bit.ly/1wPP6fn

Meanwhile, SpiNNaker (Spiking Neural Network Architecture) is a computer architecture designed by the Advanced Processor Technologies Research Group (APT) at the School of Computer Science, University of Manchester, led by Steve Furber, to simulate the human brain. It uses ARM processors in a massively parallel computing platform, based on a six-layer thalamocortical model developed by Eugene Izhikevich. SpiNNaker is being used as the Neuromorphic Computing Platform for the Human Brain Project.

And, The BrainScaleS project, a European consortium of 13 research groups is led by a team at Heidelberg University, Germany. The project aims to understand information processing in the brain at different scales ranging from individual neurons to whole functional brain areas. The research involves three approaches: (1) in vivo biological experimentation; (2) simulation on petascale supercomputers; (3) the construction of neuromorphic processors. The goal is to extract generic theoretical principles of brain function and to use this knowledge to build artificial cognitive systems. Each 20-cm-diameter silicon wafer in the system contains 384 chips, each of which implements 128,000 synapses and up to 512 spiking neurons. This gives a total of around 200,000 neurons and 49 million synapses per wafer. This allows the emulated neural networks to evolve tens-of-thousands times quicker than real time.

Qualcomm, the chip maker that powers most cell phones, calls its Zeroth chips "neural processing units," or NPUs. But this isn't the only option for neural networking. Google is building its massive brain using existing graphical processing units, or GPUs, chips originally intended for high-end video gaming.

In fact, Qualcomm expects Zeroth chips to complement, rather than replace, other processors within a device. Just as your computer probably contains both a CPU and a graphical processing unit (GPU), Qualcomm believes the computers and smartphones of the future may have all three processors. NPUs could take much of the strain off CPUs and GPUs by handling the sorts of calculations that humans or even dogs can do simply, but that vex supercomputers. That means the neuromorphic chips it's developing are still digital chips, which are more predictable and easier to manufacture than analog ones. And instead of modeling the chips as closely as possible on actual brain biology, Qualcomm's project emulates aspects of the brain's behavior. For instance, the chips encode and transmit data in a way that mimics the electrical spikes generated in the brain as it responds to sensory information.

In 2014, EMOSHAPE (www.emoshape.com) announced the launch of a major technology breakthrough with an EPU (emotional processing unit).

Thus, cognitive computers in the future may contain CPUs, GPUs, NPUs, EPUs and Quantum Processing Units (QPUs) discussed below!

Meanwhile, YDRobotics has identified the Smartphone gadget market segment as a fast and promising strategy. Taking advantage of the expensive built-in hardware in a Smartphone, its vision is to create robotic docking stations that would augment the capabilities of the device. Adding mobility and other physical capabilities, in conjunction with purposely built software (i.e., apps that give the Smartphone artificial intelligence), Smartphones will essentially become robots with boundless potential beyond that of the mere phone. "It's just a very efficient way of marketing robots to mass consumers," says CEO Artur Arsenio. "Smartphones basically have everything you need, including cameras and sensors, to turn mere things into robots."

YDream's first product is a lamp. It's a very fine desk lamp on its own, says Artur. But when you connect it to a Smartphone loaded with the requisite app, it can do everything from adjusting lighting to gauging your emotional state. As reported in Forbes, "It uses its sensors to interface socially," Artur says. "It can determine how you feel by your facial expressions and voice. In a video conference, it can tell you how participants are feeling. Or if it senses you're sad, it may Facebook your girlfriend that you need cheering up."

"Yikes. That may be a bit more interaction than you want from a desk lamp, but get used to it. Robots could intrude in ways that may seem a little off-putting at first, but that's a marker of any new technology. Moreover, says Paul Saffo, a professor at Stanford's School of Engineering and a technology forecaster of repute, the highest use of robots won't be doing old things better. It will be doing new things, things that haven't been done before, things that weren't possible before the development of key technology." [12]

As an aside, brain-to-brain communication is now on the table. An international team of scientists demonstrated what they call the first direct brain-to-brain communication, sending the words "hola" and "ciao" between two people thousands of miles apart. "We were able to directly and non-invasively transmit a thought from one person to another, without them having to speak or write," study co-author Dr. Alvaro Pascual-Leone, a neurologist at Beth Israel Deaconess Medical Center in Boston and a Harvard Medical School professor, said in a written statement. Oh my, is a brain-to-cognitive computer next up? These researchers said computers in the not-so-distant future will interact directly with the human brain in a fluent manner, supporting both computer- and brain-to-brain communication routinely. The widespread use of human brain-to-brain technologically mediated communication will create novel possibilities for human interrelation with broad social implications that will require new ethical and legislative responses. [13]

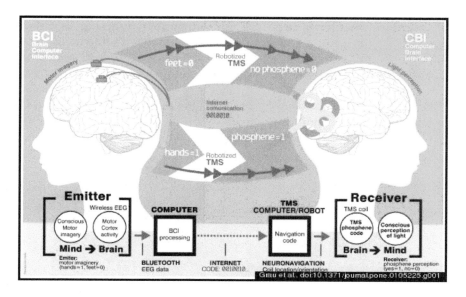

Grau et al. doi:10.1371/journal.pone.0105225.g001

The idea of quantum computing was proposed in the 1980s by physicists like Richard Feynman and David Deutsch, but it wasn't obvious that a quantum computer would be good for anything. Today's computers work by manipulating bits that exist in one of two states: a 0 or a 1. Quantum computers aren't limited to two states; they encode information as quantum bits, or qubits, that can exist in *superposition* of both 0 and 1. Qubits represent atoms, ions, photons or electrons and their respective control devices work together to act as computer *memory* and a *processor*. Because a quantum computer can contain these multiple states simultaneously, it has the potential to be millions of times more powerful than today's most powerful supercomputers.

Quantum processing units (QPUs) also utilize another aspect of quantum mechanics known as *entanglement*. One problem with the idea of quantum computers is that if you try to look at the subatomic particles, you could bump them, and thereby change their value. If you look at a qubit in superposition to determine its value, the qubit will assume the value of either 0 or 1, but not both (effectively turning your spiffy quantum computer into a mundane digital computer). To make a practical quantum computer, scientists have to devise ways of making measurements indirectly to preserve the system's integrity. Entanglement provides a potential answer. In quantum physics, if you apply an outside force to two atoms, it can cause them to become entangled, and the second atom can take on the properties of the first atom. If left alone, an atom will spin in all directions. The instant it is disturbed it chooses one spin, or one value; and at the same time, the second entangled atom will choose an opposite spin, or value. This allows scientists to know the value of the qubits without actually looking at them.

This superposition of qubits is what gives quantum computers their inherent *parallelism*. According to physicist David Deutsch, this parallelism allows a quantum computer to work on a million computations at once, while your desktop PC works on one. A 30-qubit quantum computer would equal the processing power of a conventional computer that could run at 10 teraflops (trillions of floating-point operations per second). Today's typical desktop computers run at speeds measured in gigaflops (billions of floating-point operations per second).

Okay... we are going too deep in nerdsville for this book, but for a quick overview of quantum computing watch:

Watch: Google/NASA: http://bit.ly/1fhQqw8
Quantum Computer Animated: http://bit.ly/1voALpb

D-Wave is a closely watched company in that it is perhaps the most advanced in terms of *commercializing* quantum computing, though even its founders acknowledge that they exploit only a subset of quantum mechanics, called *quantum annealing*. A universal quantum computer is one that can do any quantum computation, like Shor's factoring algorithm. D-Wave is aiming to build something much more limited.

Meanwhile, Microsoft's "Station Q" research group, set up in 2006 at the University of California, Santa Barbara, has been pursuing an unusual line in quantum computing research, called "topological quantum computing." The approach is about precisely controlling the motions of pairs of subatomic particles as they wind around one another to manipulate entangled quantum bits. These subatomic particles that the UCSB research group is trying to "braid" are known as "anyons," a type of particle that only exists in two dimensions.

In September 2014, Google announced a new research project led by physicist John Martinis from the University of California Santa Barbara (UCSB). Martinis' team will research and develop new quantum information processors based on superconducting electronics. The team at UCSB has made great strides in building superconducting quantum electronic components, and Martinis was awarded the London Prize for his "pioneering advances in quantum control and quantum information processing." If you are really interested in the design principles of quantum computers, listen to Martinis talk, "Design of a Quantum Computer." tinyurl.com/pakyjjc

While Google will now set the team to building its own quantum processor designs, the company says it will continue to collaborate with D-Wave scientists and to experiment with the "Vesuvius" machine at NASA which will be upgraded to a 1,000 qubit "Washington" processor. [14]

Google Quantum A.I. Lab
https://plus.google.com/+QuantumAILab

As we are exploring cognitive computers, The Internet of Everything poses some really significant, related hardware challenges and coping with Big Data. We've seen bits and pieces of technology that hint at the future of computing, but HP has just taken a big step toward bringing them all together. The company has unveiled "The Machine" (yes, that's the name), a processing architecture designed to cope with the flood of data from an Internet of Things. It uses clusters of special-purpose cores, rather than a few generalized cores; photonics link everything instead of slow, energy-hungry copper wires; memristors give it unified memory that's as fast as RAM yet stores data permanently, like a flash drive.

The Machine Source: HP

The result is a computer that can handle dramatically larger amounts of data, all the while using much less power. A Machine server could address 160 petabytes of data in 250 nanoseconds; HP says its hardware should be about six times more powerful than an existing server, even as it consumes 80 times less energy. Ditching older technology like copper also encourages non-traditional, three-dimensional computing shapes (you're looking at a concept here), since you're not bound by the usual distance limits. The Machine shouldn't just be for data centers and supercomputers, either—it can shrink down to laptops and phones. http://www.engadget.com/2014/06/11/hp-the-machine/[15]

SAP HANA, short for "High-Performance Analytic Appliance" is an in-memory, column-oriented, database management system developed and marketed by SAP AG. It is massively parallel, thus exploiting the maximum out of multicore processors and subsequently enabling very fast query execution. Enterra Solutions entered a global OEM agreement with SAP to integrate its Cognitive Reasoning Platform with the HANA platform. By combining the power of Enterra's Cognitive Reasoning Platform™ (CRP) with the speed and agility that SAP HANA delivers for the management of structured and unstructured data in real-time integration environments, Enterra will make rich analytics and insights available to enterprises and governmental agencies that seek to harness big-data insights to grow their businesses.

"Companies are ready for new forms of analytics," said Stephen DeAngelis, CEO of Enterra. "Businesses need to operate at a new cadence using new forms of data. We believe that through this new partnership with SAP and the integration of HANA into our platform, we can extend our lead in cognitive computing for companies across industry sectors. We anticipate that this will allow iconic brands to leverage data present at every level of their enterprises into actionable insights for decision-making. Today, it is not enough to answer the questions that you know to ask. We believe that it is also important to answer the questions that you do not know to ask before they become mission-critical." [16]

The Canadian government has invested $100 million in quantum computing, as seed money. The governments of Singapore and China are actively funding research. In comparison, the U.S. government has not made significant investments in quantum computing projects. Interestingly, the fastest supercomputer circa 2014 is in China.

More news on cognitive computers can be found at:
http://www.artificialbrains.com/
http://www.cognimem.com/index.php
http://www.therobotreport.com/

[1] http://www.wired.com/2013/05/neuro-artificial-intelligence/all
[2] http://bit.ly/1sI6Qve
[3] http://web.eecs.utk.edu/~itamar/Papers/DML_Arel_2010.pdf
[4] http://tinyurl.com/kuk8g8k
[5] http://bit.ly/19IJHO0
[6] http://huff.to/1mztP1S
[7] http://tinyurl.com/o43oun6
[8] http://affect.media.mit.edu
[9] http://tinyurl.com/np2jgo5
[10] http://tinyurl.com/m65ag9g
[11] http://bit.ly/WvQXtD
[12] http://goo.gl/fWg2P7
[13] http://tinyurl.com/k3fj7y9
[14] https://plus.google.com/+QuantumAILab
[15] http://www.engadget.com/2014/06/11/hp-the-machine
[16] http://tinyurl.com/p8jphcw

2. All's Changed ...
Changed Utterly!

"The future is already here – it is just not evenly distributed."
— William Gibson

Organizations have a lot to learn about the coming impact of cognitive computing, so we we'll open with an Albert Einstein quote, "Once you stop learning, you start dying."

Cognitive computing will have an enormous impact on the use of data in solving real world problems. The impact on fields like healthcare, education, finance, and legal (eDiscovery) are but examples where the power of technology has the chance to change entire industries. Some industries are likely to be negatively impacted by this type of technology, and many from these industries will resist change. What the people in these industries need to clearly understand is that with the pace of evolution in technology, change is going to happen and it has the potential to change quickly —exponentially. Understanding big data has everything to do with the process of discovery, advanced analytics and machine learning solutions that will help people in realizing that data is an asset and the data holds many of the answers to questions that improve industries.

What can be done with cognitive computing will be done. The question is "Will you be the doer or the one done in?"

This chapter reviews a cross section of industries already being affected. It is just a short list to give a feel for what's happening. If your industry isn't covered, you might want to search: "artificial intelligence" + "Your Industry."

JEOPARDY! WAKE-UP CALL
In 2011, IBM's Watson had access to 200 million pages of structured and unstructured content consuming four terabytes of disk storage including the

full text of Wikipedia, but was not connected to the Internet while playing against two reigning champs in the game, Jeopardy! When Watson won, it created a sensation. But many people probably saw it as little more than a high-tech parlor trick. Not anymore.

The ecosystem that IBM Watson is fueling shows that cognitive technology has great potential to have a major impact in the world. It's in its early days, but as the ecosystem takes off it will help usher in a new era of computing—transforming industries and, ideally, improving people's lives.

The success of IBM Watson, proving the value of cognitive computing, has fostered an ecosystem of cognitive computing start-ups. Watson is already being put to work in healthcare, financial services and retail. One company, Cognitive Scale, released its cognitive cloud platform and cognitive cloud-based industry applications in late 2014. Cognitive clouds are the next evolution of cloud computing. They are a new class of data interpretation and learning systems that weave insights and advice into the fabric of business and daily life.

Cognitive Scale's "Insights Fabric" cognitive cloud platform delivers insights-as-a-service from all types of social, public, private and device data and context signals. It helps master big data and uncover dark data (unstructured, untagged and untapped operational data) to improve decision-making, personalize consumer experiences, and create profitable relationships.

cognitivescale.com

The company's cognitive clouds fuse different data types (text, tweets, blogs, images, videos) on a massive scale and make sense of our increasingly interconnected and amazingly complex world. Sitting at the intersection of mobile, cloud, big data and analytics, these next generation intelligent cloud infrastructures help enterprises improve decision-making, personalize consumer experiences, and create profitable relationships.

Apps powered by the company's cognitive cloud can interact in a variety of ways: ask them questions, give them commands, and get them to guide you with insights and advice to improve decision-making, personalize consumer experiences, and create profitable relationships.

In May 2014, IBM acquired virtual assistant software startup Cognea, with plans to roll its capabilities into the Watson cognitive computing platform. Cognea's virtual assistants "relate to people using a wide variety of personalities—from suit-and-tie formal to kid-next-door friendly," said Mike Rhodin, senior vice president of IBM's Watson Group, in a blog post. "We believe this focus on creating depth of personality, when combined with an understanding of the users' personalities will create a new level of interaction that is far beyond today's 'talking' smartphones."

"I'm not talking about just giving the computer a simple command or asking a simple question," Rhodin said in the blog post. "That's yesterday's technology. I'm talking about more realistic conversations—everything from friendly chitchat to intense debate." The Cognea deal follows IBM's investments in Fluid, which makes a shopping assistant application, and Welltok, which develops online healthcare community sites.

To learn more about IBM's move to cognitive computing, read:

http://tinyurl.com/m79zxu4

CUSTOMER SERVICE

Going beyond Jeopardy! the Watson Engagement Advisor has the potential to bring the era of cognitive systems to the masses. Watson could help transform the way people and organizations interact over the lifetime of their relationships, completely changing the roles of customer service, a strategic Business Process.

Watson Engagement Advisor

Know me
Leverage profile data
for personalized
insight into customer
wants and needs to
contextualize
experience

Engage me
Dynamic, evidence-
based omni-channel
experiences that
adapt to customer
preferences

Customer

Empower Me
Interactive, informed natural language dialogue
that enables insights at the point of action

WATSON'S THOUGHT PROCESS:

| IT UNDERSTANDS THE REQUEST IN CONTEXT | IT GENERATES AND EXPLORES HYPOTHESES AGAINST THE DATA | IT EVALUATES THOSE HYPOTHESES BASED ON MORE DATA | IT LEARNS FROM ITSELF AS ONLY WATSON CAN DO | IT THEN SHARES WITH YOU WHAT IT "THINKS" | ALL IN SECONDS. ALL IN PLAIN ENGLISH |

Watson can transform the way people and companies interact with one another. Individual consumers can engage directly with Watson, in plain English, to get personalized answers to questions.

The Nielsen Innovation Lab, founded to advance research in advertising, intends to use Watson Engagement Advisor to explore ways it can help agencies and their clients better engage with consumers and increase the effect of their advertising and media plans.

Meanwhile, IBM and Genesys, a provider of customer experience and contact center solutions, have entered into a partnership to empower smarter customer experiences. Genesys will tap the IBM Watson cognitive computing system to transform the way brands engage clients across customer service, marketing and sales through data-driven insights and automated actions. As part of the agreement, IBM Watson and Genesys will develop a learning system that combines the Watson Engagement Advisor with the Genesys Customer Experience Platform to transform how organizations engage with their customers across customer experience touch points and channels of communication. As a

40

learning system, the Watson-enabled natural language solution learns, adapts and understands market and organizational data quickly and easily, and gets progressively smarter with use, outcomes and new pieces of information. [1]

Business Process Management (BPM) for customer service and other critical business processes such as logistics, sales, fulfillment, and manufacturing will never be the same as they are driven by smart cognitive systems with natural language processing. Uh oh! What about all those services jobs that make up 85% of employment? Will the Cogs take those jobs?

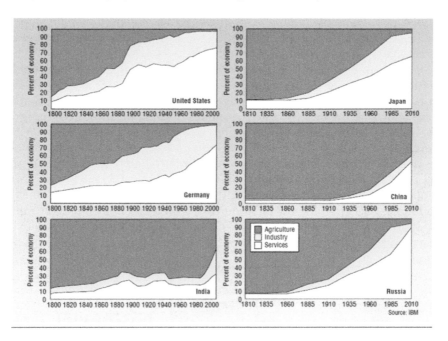

MEDICINE AND HEALTHCARE

Memorial Sloan Kettering Cancer Center, the world's oldest and largest private cancer center, has experts who have worked with an IBM team to train Watson to help assist medical professionals in choosing treatments for lung and breast cancers. The experts share their knowledge and expertise in oncology to help Watson learn everything it can about cancer care and how Memorial Sloan Kettering's experts use medical information and their experience in personalized cancer treatments.

The cognitive systems use insights gleaned from the deep experience of Memorial Sloan Kettering clinicians to provide individualized treatment options based on patient's medical information and the synthesis of a vast array of updated and vetted treatment guidelines, and published research.

The power of the technology is that it has the ability to take the information about a specific patient and match it to a huge knowledge base and history of treatment of similar patients. This process can help medical professionals gain important insights so that they can make more informed decisions, evi-

41

dence-based decisions, about what treatment to follow. Watson's ability to mine massive quantities of data means that it also keeps up, at record speeds, with the latest medical breakthroughs reported in scientific journals and meetings.

Patrick Soon-Shiong, the richest man in American medicine and founder of Nanthealth, reported to Huffington Post, "I look upon the human-patient relationship like a priest-parish relationship. I don't think there will ever, or should there ever, be the absence of human-human interaction. *I don't call it artificial intelligence. I call it amplified intelligence. We're coining this term AI3, meaning amplified, actionable and adaptive intelligence. We're going to enhance the cognitive capabilities of a human being who can't recall information at the speed and depth that we need to make the right decision.*

"But this information is in the cloud and can give the doctor actionable information in real time. With actionable, adaptive intelligence, everybody learns from everybody else. Amplified intelligence makes sure we give the right care at the right time, especially when it comes to making life-threatening decisions." Boca Raton-based Modernizing Medicine is developing a Watson-powered app, called schEMA, that's designed to help dermatologists offer optimal treatment options. One out of four dermatologists in the nation are already using Modernizing Medicine's Electronic Medical Assistant, or EMA, an iPad application to improve patient interaction and healthcare outcomes, said Daniel Cane, CEO and founder of Modernizing Medicine. As an enhancement to EMA, schEMA will combine the best of EMA's big data processing with Watson's cognitive ability to help doctors by answering medical questions at the point of care.

http://wrd.cm/1n3Oy1q

"We aren't taking the doctor out of the drivers seat," said Cane, who founded the company with Dr. Michael Sherling, a dermatologist. "We are going to make Watson the ultimate research assistant and the ultimate collaborator to help determine a course of treatment."

Based in Denver, Welltok operates CaféWell, a health optimization platform that enables people to improve their health via a combination of social networking, gaming and personalization technologies. Through Welltok's customers, which are large healthcare organizations, the service has the potential to touch the lives of more than 20 million people.

Welltok's CaféWell Concierge leverages IBM Watson to guide individuals through the process of learning about their health and modifying their life-styles. It interacts with people through text or speech, guides them to personalized activities, content and communities, volunteers suggestions, and learns about them through interactions. Individuals earn rewards, including insurance premium discounts or copay reductions, for improving their health.

The company's chief executive, Jeff Margolis, has spent nearly 20 years in the healthcare technology business, but his interest in improving the healthcare system is also personal. As a teenager, he was diagnosed with a serious illness, which led to a series of surgeries and still requires careful monitoring. "I'm on a mission," he says. "We're in the position to shift from sick care to proactively optimizing our health. Watson's an accelerator. It's groundbreaking."

Meanwhile, there is a venture capital firm that invests in research in age-related diseases, biotechnology, oncology, drug discovery, bioinformatics, personalized medicine, and regenerative medicine. The firm, Hong Kong based Deep Knowledge Ventures, has appointed a computer algorithm to its board of directors! The program, called Vital, will vote on whether to invest in a specific company or not. The algorithm looks at a range of data when making decisions, including financial information, clinical trials for particular drugs, intellectual property owned by the firm and previous funding. Of course, the idea of the algorithm voting may be just a gimmick as most large companies use Big Data search to access what is happening in the market, then the board or trusted workers can decide on the advice. Still, the PR gimmick reminds us of the growing use of cognitive computing to harness Big Data for decision making.

For more on cognitive computing in health care, visit Xerox's Palo Alto Research center's (PARC) Cognitive Computing Lab:

http://ashwinram.org/

HEALTH INSURANCE

According to the Institute of Medicine, 30 percent of the $2.3 trillion dollars spent on healthcare in the United States annually is wasted. While there are many factors contributing to this statistic, one step toward reducing waste is improving the utilization management (UM) process, which governs the preapproval of healthcare insurance coverage for many medical procedures. Improving response time, accuracy and consistency in the UM review process has been a goal of the entire industry. Attaining this goal is challenging, in part because of the volume of data that is analyzed in making UM decisions.

WellPoint teamed up with IBM on a new approach to UM: using the cognitive system IBM Watson to provide approval suggestions to medical staff based on clinical and patient data. WellPoint trained Watson with 18,000 historical cases. Now Watson uses hypothesis generation and evidence-based learning to generate confidence-scored recommendations that help healthcare professionals make decisions about utilization management. Wellpoint's Interactive Care Reviewer:

- Delivers the first cognitive computing system anticipated to streamline the review processes between a patient's physician and the patient's health plan, potentially speeding approvals from utilization management professionals, reducing waste and helping ensure evidence-based care is provided.
- Accelerates accepted testing and treatment by shortening pre-authorization approval time, which means that patients are moving forward with the first crucial step toward treatment more quickly.
- Analyzes treatment requests and matches them to WellPoint's medical policies and clinical guidelines to present consistent, evidence-based responses for clinical staff to review, in the anticipation of providing faster, better informed decisions about a patient's care.

BUSINESS NETWORKS AND BUSINESS PROCESS MANAGEMENT

Because you can no longer just manage your enterprise, but must collaborate across the entire Value Chain, there won't be one cognitive computing system at your service, there will be many, many COGs (cognitive systems) serving all the companies and customers in your adaptive Business Network that's totally Demand-driven (RIP Supply-Push). Instead of one enterprise being a command-and-control governor, think instead of connect-and-collaborate Distributed Value Creation. We're moving on from companies, or countries or people being "empires" to being virtual value creating networks, where monopolies die off as dinosaurs in the inter-dependent digital Pangaea. And, we're moving all this across national boundaries which will lead to a redefinition and role of value creation by "a nation state." One world, one value creation framework.

Watch Swiss futurist, Gerd Leonhard, on the networked economy, the networked world.

http://bit.ly/1ntXPnE

For an overview of artificial intelligence and business process management, read: *Business Process Management: The Next Wave* http://amzn.to/1uV2ugF

Special purpose COGs will interoperate via an Agent Communication Language (ACL) for multi-agent collaboration and problem solving, along with Natural Language Processing (NLP) for human interactions.

The MIT team of IBM's Cognitive Systems Institute, led by professor Thomas Malone, will concentrate on developing what it calls socio-technical tools and applications that boost the performance of groups of workers engaged in collaborative tasks, such as decision making. By more closely connecting people and computers, the MIT effort will aim for combined man-machine performance that is more intelligent than any person, group of computers can achieve alone. "As the world becomes more interconnected through the use of communications technology, it may become useful to view all the people and computers as part of a single global brain," said Malone. "It's possible that the survival of our species will depend on combining human and machine intelligence to make choices that are not just smart but are also wise." [2]

FINANCE

Major financial institutions are already working with IBM's Watson to infuse additional intelligence into their business processes. Watson is tackling data-intensive challenges across the financial services sector, including banking, financial planning and investing.

DBS Bank was formerly The Development Bank of Singapore Limited, before the present name was adopted in 2003 to reflect its changing role as a regional bank. DBS is a leading financial services group in Asia and has over 250 branches across 17 markets. Headquartered in Singapore, DBS has a growing presence in the three key Asian axes of growth, namely, Greater China, Southeast Asia and South Asia. It has earned Global Finance's "Safest Bank in Asia" accolade for five consecutive years, from 2009 to 2013.

DBS Bank's relationship managers advise their wealth-management clients by analyzing large volumes of such complex data as research reports, product information, and customer profiles. DBS uses the Watson Engagement

Advisor to analyze the relationship managers' growing corpus of investment knowledge, identify connections to customers' needs, offer better advice and determine customers' best financial options.

INDUSTRIE 4.0 AND THE INDUSTRIAL INTERNET

Industrie 4.0 is a project in the high-tech strategy of the German government, which promotes the computerization of traditional industries such as manufacturing. The goal is the intelligent factory (Smart Factory), which is characterized by adaptability, resource efficiency and ergonomics as well as the integration of customers and business partners in business and value processes. The technological basis is centered on cyber-physical systems and the Internet of Things. Experts believe that Industrie 4.0 or the "fourth industrial revolution" could be a reality in about 10 to 20 years.

Read: http://tinyurl.com/k24q6xw   Watch: http://tinyurl.com/krvjn8q

A pan-Europe group has also been formed, Horizon 2020.

http://bit.ly/Jb3s6J

Meanwhile, in the United States, the federal government has established the National Network for Manufacturing Innovation (NNMI) and other federal technology initiatives designed to strengthen the connection between U.S. manufacturing and the nation's success in inventing, innovating, producing, competing, and, ultimately, building future prosperity.

http://1.usa.gov/1xt0gK9

Another initiative known as the Smart Manufacturing Leadership Coalition (SMLC) is also working on the future of manufacturing. SMLC is a nonprofit organization of manufacturing practitioners, suppliers, and technology companies; manufacturing consortia; universities; government agencies and laboratories. The aim of this coalition is to enable stakeholders in the manufacturing industry to form collaborative R & D, implementation and advocacy groups for development of the approaches, standards, platforms and shared infrastructure that facilitate the broad adoption of manufacturing intelligence.

www.smartmanufacturingcoalition.org

Similarly, GE has been working on an initiative called "The Industrial Internet." The Industrial Internet Consortium was founded in 2014 by GE, IBM, AT&T, Intel and Cisco. The Industrial Internet aims to bring together the advances of two transformative revolutions: the myriad machines, facilities, fleets and networks that arose from the Industrial Revolution, and the more recent powerful advances in computing, information and communication systems brought to the fore by the Internet Revolution. According to GE, these developments bring together three elements that embody the essence of the Industrial Internet:

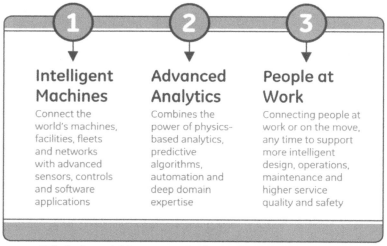

Source: GE's Industrial Internet: *Pushing the Boundaries of Minds and Machines*
http://tinyurl.com/dxu3at8

Smart self-organizing factories and supply chains are driven by *cyber-physical systems*. Despite their invisibility, embedded systems have a big role: they bring intelligence to objects, devices and other artifacts. With the emergence of high speed broadband and the Internet of Things (IoT), the embedded world is meeting the Internet world and the physical world is meeting the cyber world. In the future world of cyber physical systems, a huge number of devices connected to the physical world will be able to exchange data with each other, access Web services, and interact with people.

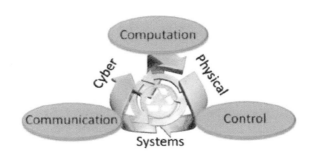

The Industrial Internet will dramatically improve productivity and efficiencies in the production process and throughout the supply chain. Processes will govern themselves, with intelligent machines and devices that can take corrective action to avoid unscheduled breakdowns of machinery. Individual parts will be automatically replenished based on real time data. Every handheld digital device in the factory will report the status of every fixed device, giving personnel mobile access to real-time, actionable information. Wearable sensors will track the location of each employee in the factory, in case of emergency.

www.iiconsortium.org and OMG, IIoT: http://tinyurl.com/oqbsdq6

New steering instruments will interlink millions of things to ensure that everything runs as planned across the entire value chain. Changes in one part of the chain, automatically trigger adjustments on the factory floor.

Customization will be automatic. Raw materials will be programmed with information that it will be part of product X, to be delivered to customer Y. Once the material is in the factory, the material itself records any deviations from the standard process, determines when it's "done," and knows how to get it to its customer.

At the warehouse level, the bright-orange Kiva robot is a boon to fledgling e-commerce companies. Created and sold by Kiva Systems, a startup that was founded in 2002 and bought by Amazon for $775 million in 2012, the robots are designed to scurry across large warehouses, fetching racks of ordered goods and delivering the products to humans who package the orders. A warehouse equipped with Kiva robots can handle up to four times as many orders as a similar unautomated warehouse, where workers might spend as much as 70 percent of their time walking about to retrieve goods. Coincidentally or not, Amazon bought Kiva soon after a press report revealed that workers at one of the retailer's giant warehouses often walked more than 10 miles a day. [3]

TRANSPORTATION AND LOGISTICS

One Google driverless car could reduce the demand for privately owned cars by a factor of 5 to 10. Google isn't the only one getting into driverless cars. Tesla Motors, American maker of electric cars and drive trains and Baidu, the Chinese search company, have also entered the fray. Meanwhile, logistics and supply chain management will never be the same, especially as Amazon's Prime Air and Google's Project Wing delivery drones take flight (regulators permitting). [4]

Occupation	Number of Workers
Transportation	3,628,000
Retail salespersons	3,286,000
First line supervisors	3,132,000
Cashiers	3,109,000
Secretaries	3,082,000

Going beyond the impact of driverless cars on the employment of taxi drivers, watch out, you millions of truck drivers (currently the number one occupation, outside of the military, for men in the U.S.). By the way, ship captain, the self-sailing ship is up next! Unmanned drone ships could become a reality on our oceans within the decade, according to Rolls-Royce.

LEGAL PROFESSIONS

Let's consider the implications of law firms with this futuristic account by Jeffrey Brandt in LegalIT Professional Magazine. "Welcome to the global law firm of DLA, Watson, & Siri. The year is 2065. I am Stevie, a Mark 3 Siri assistant. It is my task to acquaint you with the history and functioning of the firm.

"Many things have changed in the legal industry since the end of the first decade of 2000. As a law firm this has forced us to review all aspects of our personnel, our processes and our technology. We practice in all areas of law around the world.

"We're a smaller firm since the de-equitizing of 38% of our partners in 2019. Our clients want only the best in legal talent and our senior lawyers are the best at what they do. We did not start to eliminate support staff positions until our first Watson came online in 2014. It wasn't until our third Watson AI came on line and Apple released the Siri Mark 4 upgrades that the firm chose to eliminate the bulk of paralegal and staff positions. It should be noted that our law firm is the only law firm in the world currently running ten intercommunicating Watson AI units." [5]

"Robert Cannon, law expert, predicts that everything that can be automated will be automated. In the law office, the clerks who used to prepare discovery have been replaced by software. IBM Watson is replacing researchers by reading every report ever written anywhere. This begs the question: What can the human contribute? The short answer is that if the job is one where that question cannot be answered positively, that job is not likely to exist."

TRANSCRIPTIONISTS OBSOLETE

Powered by IBM's Watson, "conversation flowers" placed on tables automatically identify speakers by voice and generate real-time transcripts of conversations, rendering transcriptionists obsolete.

Here's a March 2014 account from a professional transcriber, Isaac. "A couple of years ago I contacted Baynes (a Ukrainian Mathematics graduate student at Kiev University who moonlights as an app creator on Elance), to create an interactive transcript app. I sent Baynes a 1 hour one-on-one Skype interview. The audio quality was not that great and the line dropped a few times during the interview. I struggled to transcribe this particular interview. Ten minutes later, he sent me a transcript of the interview. I compared his transcript to my transcript using the compare feature in MS Word. The transcript was 98.32% accurate! And it only took him 10 minutes to transcribe an audio. It took me 6 hours.

"I was stunned. I had a moment of derealization. I realized that my days as an academic transcriber are numbered. What to do!

"Yesterday I got in touch with Baynes, after a few days brooding. I had one question for him, 'how long before the app hits the market?' 'A year at most,' was what he told me. So I have until April 1st 2015 to learn a new skill. And I need to learn something that's Watson-proof. Any ideas?" [6]

By placing an IBM "conversation flower" on a table during a meeting and using audio and video processing, the device would be able to identify specific speakers by their voice and appearance and automatically create a transcript, correctly identifying whoever is speaking. The device also opens like a flower when the conversation becomes vibrant and animated.

JOURNALISM: WHO WROTE THIS BOOK?

Wouldn't it have been neat if I could have turned the job of researching and writing this book to a Cog? I thought about it, but I thought the Cog would want the royalties!

The Associated Press robot-written stories have arrived. AP announced in June 2014 that it would start using the technology to produce significantly more earnings reports. Managing Editor Lou Ferrara said the stories began to appear around the middle of July, and all the ones you're seeing right now have been checked by human eyes. "The tap isn't fully open yet," he said. Some stories were published just as Automated Insights filed them, others have had a few "bugs here and there," Ferrara said. "What I'm trying to get out of is the data processing business," Ferrara told Poynter earlier this month. "I can't have journalists spending a ton of time data processing stuff. Instead I need them reporting." [7]

An Automated Insights' Story

Meanwhile, Narrative Sciences, a company with an artificial intelligence product called Quill can turn data (e.g., spreadsheets) into stories that read as if they were written by a human. This has instantly obvious applications in the business world. Why isn't a certain product selling? Why is a particular retail franchise succeeding or failing? Quill can spin wonky stats into a story that anyone can read so that they can answer these questions without having to dive into alternately boring or scary numbers.

RETAIL AND eCOMMERCE

Headline in Venturebeat: "Why Retrevo thinks it can outsell Amazon.com." Retrevo.com is one of the largest consumer electronics shopping and review sites in the world. In retail settings, cognitive systems are used to consider past buying patterns, inventory, order management, supply chain and other customer relationship management issues that target individual buyers. Here, mistaken recommendations will not count against a cognitive system, since people are accustomed to "irrational" buying patterns due to issues such as brand loyalty, which transcends rational analysis, according to principal scientist Aditya Vailaya at Retrevo Inc.

"This new kind of AI driven, content-commerce marketplace will require a new level of transparency among retailers, as it would be tempting for some to change their recommendation based on the inventory they hold. We at Retrevo maintain this transparency by showing "Add to Cart" where a product will result in a good ownership experience. And we added the world's first-ever "Do Not Add To Cart" button – proof that we really have the consumer's best interest at heart. Whenever Retrevo's AI system deems a product a "bad buy," a "Do Not Add to Cart" button will appear next to it." [8]

An expert store associate doesn't just answer a shopper's questions, he digs for more details in order to come up with the best product suggestions and advice he can give her. Digital agency Fluid Inc. is working to bring that capability to a shopping app, leveraging the technology of IBM's Watson to do so, says Fluid CEO Kent Deverell.

Fluid's prototype of the Watson-powered app, called the Fluid Expert Personal Shopper, works with the outdoors gear and apparel retailer, The North Face. The North Face is one of several brands owned by VF Corp., which is No. 113 in the Internet Retailer Top 500 Guide. With the app, a North Face shopper could speak or type into an iPad a question such as, "I'm going on an expedition to Patagonia. What gear should I bring?" Then Watson, via the app, asks questions to refine what she needs, perhaps to find when she is going or how many miles she plans to trek per day. If the shopper says her expedition is planned for the winter, for example, Watson may suggest she look for a backpack with ABS, an airbag-based avalanche rescue system used by winter athletes.

PERSONAL ASSISTANT

An intelligent personal assistant is a mobile software agent that can perform tasks for, or deliver services to, an individual based on user input, location awareness, and the ability to access information from a variety of online sources (such as weather or traffic conditions, news, stock prices, retail prices, etc.). Examples of such an agent are Cognitive Code's SILVIA, Samsung's S Voice, LG's Voice Mate, Google Now, Microsoft Cortana, HTC's Hidi and Apple's Siri.

Sure, you've heard of Siri. But where did it come from? After giving us the Internet (ARPANET), the U.S. military struck again with CALO. CALO was an artificial intelligence project that attempted to integrate numerous AI technologies into a cognitive assistant. CALO is an acronym for "Cognitive Assistant that Learns and Organizes." The name was inspired by the Latin word "calonis," which means "soldier's servant." The project started in May 2003 and ran for five years, ending in 2008. (Wikipedia).

The CALO effort has had many major spin-offs, most notably the Siri intelligent software assistant that is now part of the Apple iOS; Social Kinetics, a social application that learned personalized intervention and treatment strategies for chronic disease patients, sold to RedBrick Health; the Trapit project, which is a Web scraper and news aggregator that makes intelligent selections of web content based on user preferences; Tempo AI, a smart calendar; Desti, a personalized travel guide; and Kuato Studios, a game development startup.

CALO was funded by the Defense Advanced Research Projects Agency (DARPA) under its Personalized Assistant that Learns (PAL) program. DARPA's five-year contract brought together over 300 researchers from 25 of the top university and commercial research institutions, with the goal of building a new generation of cognitive assistants that can reason, learn from experience, be told what to do, explain what they are doing, reflect on their experience, and respond robustly to surprise. SRI International was the lead integrator responsible for coordinating the effort to produce an assistant that can live with and learn from its users, provide value to them, and then pass a yearly evaluation that measures how well the system has learned to do its job.

In 2012, *Popular Science* awarded its "Innovation of the Year" to Google Now. The publication praised Google's voice-enabled personal assistant/psychic stalker app as "the first virtual assistant that truly anticipates your needs" and singled out the way it "quietly keeps track of searches, calendar events, locations, and travel patterns." *Popular Science* also couldn't resist throwing a jab at Apple's Siri voice assistant, which it said seemed "outdated" compared to Google Now.

Startup Viv Labs, founded by Siri's creators Dag Kittlaus, Adam Cheyer, and Chris Brigham back at SRI, is currently working on its AI system called Viv. Viv founders say you'll access its artificial intelligence as a utility, the way you draw on electricity. Simply by speaking, you will connect to what they are calling "a global brain." And that brain can help power a million different apps and devices.

Viv differs from Siri and Google Now in that it can analyze different nouns in your sentence independently to compile an accurate and useful answer. This means you can ask Viv more long winded and complicated requests while speaking naturally as you would to another person.

For example, Siri or Google Now wouldn't be able to help you with a request like "On my way to my brother's house, I need to pick up some cheap wine that goes well with lasagna," which *Wired* magazine cites as an example. Those services would be able to pick out a liquor store for you that's en route to your brother's house, but probably wouldn't be able to pair a specific wine that goes well with lasagna. Viv, however, breaks down the sentence into three key parts: Lasagna, brother, and home. It recognizes that lasagna is a food item, that your brother is a person and that home is an address. It then pulls together a bunch of resources such as Google contacts, Wine.com, Mapquest, and Recipe Puppy to answer all parts of the request. For example, it uses the information from Recipe Puppy to learn about the ingredients in lasagna, and then parses through compatible wines using a platform like Wine.com.

Viv also gets smarter as more people use it. Ultimately, the team seeks to create a digital assistant that knows what you want without having to issue a specific command. The end result will be a digital assistant who knows what you want before you ask for it. For instance, if you say "I'm drunk" to your phone, Viv would automatically call your favorite car service to take you home.

As reported in *Wired*,[9] Viv is an open system that will let innumerable businesses and applications become part of its boundless brain. The technical barriers are minimal, requiring brief "training" (in some cases, minutes) for Viv to understand the jargon of the specific topic. As Viv's knowledge grows, so will its understanding; its creators have designed it based on three principles they call its "pillars": It will be taught by the world, it will know more than it is taught, and it will learn something every day. As with other AI products, that teaching involves using sophisticated algorithms to interpret the language and behavior of people using the system—the more people use it, the smarter it gets. By knowing who its users are and which services they interact with, Viv can sift through that vast trove of data and find new ways to connect and manipulate the information. The end result will be a digital assistant who knows what you want before you ask for it!

Let's go beyond the personal assistant and on to the "Family Assistant." As reported in *Wired*, "For many families, the tablet has become the central, shared computing device in the home. It's a hub for learning, for entertainment, and for staying connected. But what if your tablet was even more interactive? What if it woke up when you came home, recognized your face, and suggested a couple of things you might want for dinner? What if, when asked a question, it could tailor its answer directly to you, instead of just offering a blanket response? Watch MIT's Dr. Cynthia Breazeal introduce Jibo, the family robot.

Meet Jibo: http://www.myjibo.com/
Read more about Jibo at http://wrd.cm/1mhxZLS

Smart Process Apps: Siri Meets Watson

The Apple App Store has thousands of business apps that are barely used. The main reason? They lack a process layer. They do not interact well with existing information and processes. So enter Smart Process Apps (SPAs) and a new era of competitive advantage in business. Unlike ordinary mobile apps, SPAs integrate and leverage core business systems. SPAs bring order and auditability to chaotic, unstructured, interdependent and extended processes that are currently executed primarily via email, spreadsheets and meetings. The goal of Smart Process Apps is to improve this messy range of human-based activities.

Doug Henschen wrote in *Information Week*, "Siri and Watson are both pretty smart cookies, but they travel in wildly different circles. Siri's all fashionable and socially connected while Watson's all down to business, hobnobbing with healthcare, insurance, and banking bigwigs. Imagine what a power couple they could be." The Apple-IBM alliance announced in 2014 is, as many have observed, a complementary combination of a consumer powerhouse and a business behemoth. The obvious hope is that they will be better together. Apple gives IBM the most fashionable consumer devices and mobile experience available. IBM can take that experience into the enterprise and add a Mobile-First Platform for iOS with the promise of more than 100 smart apps.

http://amzn.to/1rmzUa9

THE FREELANCE WORK FORCE

"We believe Watson is going to be huge," said Elance CEO Fabio Rosati. "It's going to be the next big thing after the Internet." Elance has a vested interest, since it will create specialized cloud services to assist app developers in accessing a pool of more than three million freelancers, many of whom will complete an IBM Watson certification program."

Elance was first launched in 1999, its name inspired by a 1998 *Harvard Business Review* article titled "The Dawn of the E-Lance Economy." It was initially developed as a technology for supporting virtual work. Two years later Elance introduced a vendor management system (VMS) for contractors and third-party services used by large enterprises. In 2006, Elance sold its enterprise software division and developed instead its current web-based platform for online, contingent work.

Elance is used by about 500,000 businesses and 2 million registered freelance professionals, who have collectively earned nearly $850 million to date. A merger with oDesk, another online staffing platform, was confirmed in December 2013. The deal is expected to create a resource that consists of 8 million freelancers and 2 million businesses.

MILITARY TRANSITIONS TO CIVILIAN LIFE

We discussed affective computing in Chapter 1. Now, let's look at an application for military personnel. The United Services Automobile Association (USAA) is a Fortune 500 financial services group offering banking, investing, and insurance to people and families that serve, or served, in the United States military. At the end of 2013, there were 10.1 million members. And now it's going to work on helping military service members understand the nuances of the financial transition back to civilian life.

A lot of what USAA does is inevitably answering complicated questions from servicemen and women transitioning back into civilian life. It's estimated that 155,000 military members make the change every year. That's a lot of questions to field. Transitioning military members can visit usaa.com or use a mobile browser to "Ask Watson" questions specific to leaving the military, such as "What is the best way to write a resume?" or "How do I make the most of the Post-9/11 GI Bill?" As a result, Watson combs through volumes of USAA's business data to provide answers to members' inquiries with confidence while gaining value and experience over time. Watson has analyzed more than 3,000 specialized military transition documents, so it knows all the rules and regulations about how to make the change. And its natural language processing allows it to understand real questions asked in diverse ways. That way, even if someone doesn't know how to ask a question in the optimal way, the IBM Watson Engagement Advisor can still attempt to parse the meaning at the heart of what they're saying. [10]

"The computer will see you now" is an article in the *Economist* magazine. "Ellie is a psychologist, and a damned good one at that. Smile in a certain way, and she knows precisely what your smile means. Develop a nervous tic or tension in an eye, and she instantly picks up on it. She listens to what you say, processes every word, works out the meaning of your pitch, your tone, your posture, everything. She is at the top of her game but, according to a new study, her greatest asset is that she is not human.

 Read: http://tinyurl.com/pjr388g   Watch: http://bit.ly/1t9kXUz

"When faced with tough or potentially embarrassing questions, people often do not tell doctors what they need to hear. Yet the researchers behind Ellie, led by Jonathan Gratch at the University of Southern California Institute for Creative Technologies in Los Angeles, suspected from their years of monitoring human interactions with computers that people might be more willing to talk if presented with an avatar. This quality of encouraging openness and honesty, Dr. Gratch believes, will be of particular value in assessing the psychological problems of soldiers—a view shared by America's Defense Advanced Research Projects Agency, which is helping to pay for the project.

"Soldiers place a premium on being tough, and many avoid seeing psychologists at all costs. That means conditions such as post-traumatic stress disorder (PTSD), to which military men and women are particularly prone, often get dangerous before they are caught. Ellie could change things for the better by confidentially informing soldiers with PTSD that she feels they could be a risk to themselves and others, and advising them on how to seek treatment." 11

SMARTER SERIOUS GAMES FOR BUSINESS

"While *complying* can be an effective strategy for physical survival, it's a lousy one for personal fulfilment. Living a satisfying life requires more than simply meeting the demands of those in control. Yet in our offices and our classrooms we have way too much compliance and way too little engagement. The former might get you through the day, but only the latter will get you through the night." —Dan Pink, author of *Drive*

Phaedra Boinodiris is the Serious Games Program Manager at IBM. She has been introducing Watson AI into serious games, including talent management. IBM's Assessment testing solutions provide the Big Data that correlates to an employee's hard and soft skill sets. This Big Data informs the creation of a unique personal avatar; a unique visual representation of his or her resume. IBM's analytics engine powered by Watson algorithms has created avatars into a tailored origami shape, with patterns, colors and shapes that match to where employees are in their career progression.

 http://amzn.to/1plb84A

Employees can then be matched to a set of mentors and projects that fit where they are in their career journeys. They will have many choices in terms of how to advance their careers, but it is up to them to choose which direction and to take the action to get there. Like a Role Playing Game (RPG), these evolution trees are displayed visually and show where investments in training and

KPI goal completion need to occur in order to "level up." Mentors are matched at every level of evolution to coach and guide each employee as they level-up their avatar. As each employee progresses, changes can be updated throughout the community in real time, continuously altering the opportunities for the employee as well as his or her community status.

In this way, employees are more accurately matched to the right projects at the right time. Each employee is constantly aware of the training and skills they need in order to unlock their next set of projects and career milestones. No longer will critical decisions such as project staffing, mentor matching, and hiring be made arbitrarily. By using game technologies, organizations can give employees a needed sense of self direction and empowerment, while gaining a more holistic view of employees' skills, gaps, and interests.

SMARTER SERIOUS GAMES FOR THE MILITARY

Watson goes to war. Intelligence powered gaming can disrupt the entire way that missions are planned, organized, trained for and vetted. Gaming environment can facilitate strategic assessment of force policy, cascading effects of decisions made based on policy as well as specific battlefield scenarios. Game strategy can be service or joint forces based; joint games can reduce silo thinking. Game investments have previously focused on skills training and not on games that enable Strategic Execution or Tactical Operations. These latter types of games require a complex infrastructure that is based on the cascading rules contained in doctrine. A Strategic Execution or a Tactical Operations game would allow each Mission plan component to be vetted, stressed, and prioritized by the entire decision and action chain.

Imagine the creation of a Multi-player Real-Time Strategy game (MRTS), played at the Commander level that can generate likely scenarios and cascading effects based on real-life hypotheses. Data gathered from stimulus-response exercises can help model how enemies adapt to space and time conditions, current event data, and the positioning of friendly troops and military assets.

Watson powered Smarter Serious Games allow players to play in an environment that exploits hypotheses made about the real world, enabling the vetting and optimization of strategy. War fighters can evaluate and re-evaluate the consequences of decisions, issuing or retracting commands in the past, present, and future, blurring the boundary between hypothetical and committed decisions. In particular, the player can revisit critical decision points, learn what decisions had the most long-term impact, and use statistical information on the timeline to make more informed decisions.

ANALYTICS FOR EVERYONE AND THE DEBATER

The new Cognitive Watson Analytics can ingest spreadsheets and data from Salesforce, Teradata and Oracle systems to start making connections and answering questions in a natural language format. A marketing pro can ask about what campaigns are delivering the most returns; a HR leader can find data about a retention; and a sales person can find out about deals that'll close soon. In some respects, IBM is trying to push microanalytics via what it calls a "single business analytics experience."

The first release of Watson Analytics includes a *freemium* version of its cloud-based service designed to run on desktop and mobile devices. Watson Analytics offers a full range of self-service analytics, including access to easy-to-use data refinement and data warehousing services that make it easier for business users to acquire and prepare data, beyond simple spreadsheets, for analysis and visualization that can be acted upon and interacted with.

IBM Watson Analytics uses natural language to make interaction with powerful, predictive analytics easier with the ability to understand key questions, such as:

- What are the key drivers of my product sales?
- Which benefits drive employee retention the most?
- Which deals are most likely to close?

Okay, powerful analytics are required today, but how about debating the results? When asked to discuss any topic, the Watson Debater can autonomously scan its knowledge database for relevant content, "understand" the data, and argue both for and against a topic. Watson can list, without human assistance, what it believes are the most valid arguments for and against a topic of choice —in natural language.

http://tinyurl.com/ka8onkt

THE NEW COGNITIVE COMPUTING CURRICULUM

When I began my career in computing in 1967, very few universities had computer science curriculums. Wow, has that changed! And now there's a new curriculum on the block. IBM's Watson cognitive computing system is finding its way into the classroom at some of the nation's top technology-oriented educational institutions. Big Blue announced that it is partnering with some of the country's leading technology universities to launch cognitive computing courses that give students access via the cloud to Watson. Enrollment opened in the fall 2014 for cognitive computing courses at Carnegie Mellon University, New York University (NYU), The Ohio State University, Rensselaer Polytechnic Institute (RPI), University of California, Berkeley, University of Michigan and the University of Texas in Austin.

"All of the courses are designed to be hands-on and project-based, like mine at Michigan. Each class will get access to a version of Watson delivered as a cloud service," said David Chesney, a computer science professor at the University of Michigan, in a post on IBM's "Building a Smarter Planet" blog. "Classmates will split up into teams, identify uses for Watson, develop apps and also write business plans—as if they're entrepreneurs creating startups. Think of it as Silicon Valley in the classroom." [12]

You may want to track the Cognitive Systems Institute, a collaborative effort between universities, research institutes, and IBM clients to advance the state-of-the-art in cognitive computing.

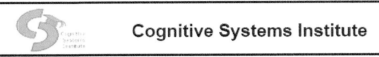

http://www.linkedin.com/groups/Cognitive-Systems-Institute-6729452

THE COGNITIVE INTERNET OF EVERYTHING

Cisco estimates that 50 billion devices and objects will be connected to the Internet by 2020. Yet today, more than 99 percent of things in the physical world remain unconnected. The growth and convergence of processes, data, and things on the Internet will make networked connections more relevant and valuable than ever before, creating unprecedented opportunities for industries, businesses, and people.

Ant-sized radios could help connect *trillions* of devices to the Internet of Things. A team of researchers from Stanford University and the University of California, Berkeley, has created prototype radio-on-a-chip communications devices that are powered by ambient radio waves. Comprising receiving and transmitting antennas and a central processor, the completely self-contained ant-sized devices are very cheap to manufacture, don't require batteries to run and could give the "Internet of Things" (IoT) exponential growth.

From a technical viewpoint, the prototype is a self-contained transceiver module with an in-built central processor designed to interpret and execute instructions, powered from the energy scavenged from ambient radio waves. Highlighting its low energy consumption, the researchers say that a single AAA battery, if it were hooked up, would keep it running for more than a century.

The IoT is the next technology transition when devices will allow us to sense and control the physical world. But, it's also part of something even bigger. The Internet of Everything (IoE) is the networked connection of *people, process, data,* and *things.* Its benefit is derived from the compound impact of these connections and the value it creates as "everything" comes online.

As noted BPM expert, Jim Sinur, wrote in his blog, "In advanced situations resources can collaborate in a machine to machine (M2M) fashion, a human to human fashion (H2H), a human to machine fashion (H2M) or a machine to human fashion (M2H). All of these styles can interact with each other to accomplish business outcomes. The type and amount of intelligent business operations that can be created by the combination of process and the IoT is now being expanded to the Internet of Everything." The IT analyst firm, Gartner, describes the Internet of Everything as a combination of:

- Internet of Information – the traditional World Wide Web
- Internet of Systems – network of business and consumer applications
- Internet of People – network of relationships in social networks
- Internet of Places – commercial and public places as Internet nodes
- Internet of Things – connected physical devices with sensors
- Internet of Virtual Entities – "intelligent" digital entities

H2M, M2H? In a *Time* magazine article, "Never Offline," Lev Grossman and Matt Vella write, "What might post-humanity be like? The paradox of a wearable device is that it both gives you control and takes it away at the same time. Consider the watch's fitness applications. They capture all data that your body generates, your heart and activity and so on, gathers it up and stores and returns it to you in a form you can use. Once the development community gets through 'apping' it, there's no telling what else it might gather. This will change your experience of your body. The wristwatch made the idea of not knowing what time it was seem bizarre; in five years it might seem bizarre not to know how many calories you've eaten today, or what your resting heart rate is."

BPM pioneer, Setrag Khoshafian, wrote "The coordination and execution of connected devices will need a context. They will also need collaboration to achieve specific goals. The increasingly intelligent things, together with human participants, need to have their tasks orchestrated to achieve business objectives. Furthermore, the intelligence that is mined from Big Data needs to be made actionable—again in the context of specific business solutions. Enter the 'Process of Everything.'" As Khoshafian indicates, the unfolding world is not just about the Internet of Everything, it's also the "Process of Everything," and those processes will be built on distributed intelligence, distributed to each and every entity with built in cognitive capabilities to learn, think and act autonomously in a multi-agent environment of complex adaptive systems.

Current research on Internet of Things (IoT) mainly focuses on how to enable general objects to see, hear, and smell the physical world for themselves, and make them connected to share the observations. In the paper, *Cognitive Internet of Things: A New Paradigm beyond Connection*, the researchers argue that *only connected* is not enough, beyond that, general objects should have the capability to learn, think, and understand both physical and social worlds by themselves. Here's an excerpt, "Cognitive Internet of Things (CIoT) is a new network paradigm, where (physical/ virtual) things or objects are interconnected and behave as agents, with minimum human intervention, the things interact with each other following a context-aware perception-action cycle, use the methodology of understanding-by-building to learn from both the physical environment and social networks, store the learned semantic and/or knowledge in kinds of databases, and adapt themselves to changes or uncertainties via resource-efficient decision-making mechanisms, with two primary objectives in mind:

- bridging the physical world (with objects, resources, etc) and the social world (with human demand, social behavior, etc), together with themselves to form an intelligent physical-cyber-social (iPCS) system;
- enabling smart resource allocation, automatic network operation, and intelligent service provisioning."

"Generally, CIoT serves as a transparent bridge between physical world (with general physical/virtual things, objects, resources, etc.) and social world (with human demand, social behavior, etc.), together with itself to form an intelligent physical-cyber-social (iPCS) system. With a synthetic methodology learning-by-understanding located at the heart, the framework of CIoT includes five fundamental cognitive tasks: Perception-action cycle, Massive data analytics, Semantic derivation and knowledge discovery, Intelligent decision-making, and On-demand service provisioning."

Read the paper here: http://arxiv.org/pdf/1403.2498v1.pdf

The First International Conference on Cognitive Internet of Things Technologies kicked off in October, 2014 in Rome, Italy. M.I.T PhD and YDreams Robotics CEO, Artur Arsénio keynote was "The Internet of Intelligent Things - Bringing Intelligence into Objects."

http://coiot.org/2014/show/home

Saffron Technology, headquartered in Cary, North Carolina, develops cognitive computing systems that use incremental learning to understand and unify by entity (person, place or thing) the connections between an entity and other "things" in data, along with the context of their connections and their raw frequency counts. This approach provides a semantic and statistical representation of knowledge. Saffron learns from all sources of data including structured and unstructured data to support knowledge-based decision making. Its technology captures the connections between data points at the entity level and stores these connections in an associative memory. Similarity algorithms and predictive analytics are then combined with the associative index to identify patterns in the data.

Saffron Technology deploys an associative memory, or "natural learning" approach, that finds connections among data across diverse sources, without the need for rules or modeling, while learning incrementally and anticipating outcomes based on patterns it finds in the data. Designed to be easily integrated with existing investments and initiatives, Saffron 10 ingests data natively from all legacy file systems, making it seamless for businesses to apply the power of Saffron to other applications.

saffron www.saffrontech.com

"Saffron 10 is hastening our vision of powering *the Intelligence of Every 'Thing.'* The explosion of devices and sensors require a next generation of data sense making tools squarely focused on separating the signal from the noise, allowing users to not just see important patterns, but anticipate and adapt on-the-fly as new information arrives," said Saffron CEO Gayle Sheppard. "By combining these composite memories with a deep understanding of time and sequence, Saffron is enabling far more accurate risk analysis, personalization, fraud detection, and other solutions that were previously limited by static data modeling and non-temporal understanding," continued Sheppard.

---

[1] eWeek: http://tinyurl.com/pdyxdf7
[2] http://www.eetimes.com/document.asp?doc_id=1319693
[3] http://bit.ly/1cb2sqn
[4] http://reut.rs/1ooUCQQ
[5] http://tinyurl.com/luf7rge
[6] http://bit.ly/1q8ljJ0
[7] http://tinyurl.com/mvdmquq
[8] http://venturebeat.com/2011/03/17/retrevo-electronic-retail/
[9] http://www.wired.com/2014/08/viv/
[10] Slate: http://tinyurl.com/ndr9ghy
[11] http://tinyurl.com/ko7tngj
[12] eWeek: http://tinyurl.com/n2w9wjl

3. Whither Mankind: Symbiosis or Genocide

"It's hard to make predictions, especially about the future," —Yogi Berra.

Consider Google's acquisition of DeepMind that came with an estimated $400 million price tag and an unusual stipulation that adds extra gravity —and a dose of reality to this thing we call cognitive computing. Google agreed to create an AI safety and ethics review board to ensure that the technology is developed safely. "Eventually, I think human extinction will probably occur, and technology will likely play a part in this," DeepMind's Shane Legg said. Among all forms of technology that could wipe out the human species, he singled out artificial intelligence, or AI, as the "number 1 risk for this century."

Let's give it up for a minute to James Barrat, author of *Our Final Invention*. "Artificial Intelligence helps choose what books you buy, what movies you see, and even who you date. It's in your smart phone, your car, and it has the run of your house. It makes most of the trades on Wall Street, and controls our transportation, energy, and water infrastructure. Artificial Intelligence is for the 21st century what electricity was for the 20th and steam power for the 19th.

"But there's one critical difference — electricity and steam will never out-think you.

"The Hollywood cliché that artificial intelligence will take over the world could soon become scientific reality as AI matches, then surpasses human intelligence. *Each year AI's cognitive speed and power doubles — ours does not.* Corporations and government agencies are pouring billions into achieving AI's Holy Grail — human-level intelligence. Scientists argue that AI that advanced will have survival drives much like our own. Can we share the planet with it and survive?"

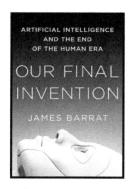

 http://tinyurl.com/q7obkjf

According to Louis Del Monte, physicist and author of *The Artificial Intelligence Revolution: Will Artificial Intelligence Serve Us Or Replace Us?*, the real danger occurs when self-aware machines realize they share the planet with humans. They "might view us the same way we view harmful insects" because humans are a species that "is unstable, creates wars, has weapons to wipe out the world twice over, and makes computer viruses." http://read.bi/UkiZ9K

The International Committee for Robot Arms Control (ICRAC) is a Non Governmental Organization (NGO). It's an international committee of experts in robotics technology, robot ethics, international relations, international security, arms control, international humanitarian law, human rights law, and public campaigns, concerned about the pressing dangers that military robots pose to peace and international security and to civilians in war. http://icrac.net/

Ryan Calo, assistant professor of law at the University of Washington believes that robotic technology is advancing so rapidly with such heavyweight implications that the current structure of the US government will be ill-equipped to handle it. Speaking at the Aspen Ideas Festival, he called for the creation of a new governmental agency, the Federal Robotics Commission (FRC) that would oversee the safe development and maintenance of new robotic applications. Read his paper on the subject at:
http://tinyurl.com/m8xvwzb
Listen to his argument in 2 minutes: http://bit.ly/XEjNIj

This has happened in the past for other breakthrough technologies — just consider the FCC for radio, the FAA for aircraft, the FDA for various foods and drugs. The list goes on, but it currently leaves robots unaddressed. If the U.S. won't do it for safety reasons, Calo argues we should do it for innovation reasons: "Other countries are getting serious about robotics policy. If we don't, this will be the first form of technology since steam where America did not have a leading role." http://www.businessinsider.com/ryan-calo-on-robot-regulation-2014-7

Entrepreneur and inventor Elon Musk, founder of Tesla, Solar City, and SpaceX, took to Twitter to sound the alarm about the dangers of artificial intelligence: "Worth reading Superintelligence by Bostrom. We need to be super careful with AI. Potentially more dangerous than nukes." Watch: Elon Musk: "With artificial intelligence we are summoning the demon."

 http://tinyurl.com/mef2qgr

 http://amzn.to/1DOzKfX

Here is an informative Amazon review of Bostrom's book, "Not surprisingly, 200+ pages later, the author can't answer the 'what is to be done' question concerning the likely emergence of non-human (machine-based) super-intelligence, sometime, possibly soon. This is expected because, as a species, we've always been the smartest ones around and never had to even think about the possibility of coexistence alongside something or someone impossibly smart and smart in ways well beyond our comprehension, possibly driven by goals we can't understand and acting in ways that may cause our extinction.

"Building his arguments on available data and extrapolating from there, Bostrom is confident that:

- some form of self-aware, machine super-intelligence is likely to emerge
- we may be unable to stop it, even if we wanted to, no matter how hard we try
- while we may be unable to stop the emergence of super-intelligence, we could prepare ourselves to manage it and possibly survive it
- our not taking this seriously and not being prepared may result in our extinction while serious pre-emergence debate and preparation may result in some form of co-existence

"It's radical and perhaps frightening but our failure to comprehend the magnitude of the risks we are about to confront would be a grave error given that, once super-intelligence begins to manifest itself and act, the change may be extremely quick and we may not be afforded a second chance."

In a BBC interview, renowned Professor, Stephen Hawking was answering questions regarding his new speech synthesizer, which includes rudimentary artificial intelligence. He said, 'The development of full artificial intelligence could spell the end of the human race. It would take off on its own, and re-design itself at an ever increasing rate. Humans, who are limited by slow biological evolution, couldn't compete, and would be superseded." [1]

Read: http://tinyurl.com/p5t73je Watch: http://tinyurl.com/nyd4xr2

Watch the luddites' futile resistance in the trailer to *Transcendence* ...

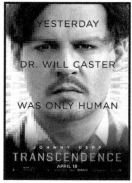

http://tinyurl.com/keg9cdw

THE POST-WORK SOCIETY

Tom Standage, digital editor for *The Economist*, makes the point that the next wave of technology is likely to have a more profound impact than those that came before it: "Robots and AI threaten to make even some kinds of skilled work obsolete (e.g., legal clerks). This will displace people in service roles, and the income gap between skilled workers whose jobs cannot be automated and everyone else will widen. This is a recipe for instability."

In September 2013 economist Carl Benedikt Frey and information engineer Michael A. Osborne, both at the University of Oxford, published a study titled "The Future of Employment" [2] estimating the probability that 702 occupations would soon be computerized out of existence. Their findings were startling. "Advances in data mining, machine vision, artificial intelligence and other technologies could, they argued, put 47 percent of American jobs at high risk of being automated in the years ahead. Loan officers, tax preparers, cashiers, locomotive engineers, paralegals, roofers, taxi drivers and even animal breeders are all in danger of going the way of the switchboard operator." In their report they write, "While computerization has been historically confined to routine tasks involving explicit rule-based activities, algorithms for big data are now rapidly entering domains reliant upon pattern recognition and can readily substitute for labor in a wide range of non-routine cognitive tasks. In addition, advanced robots are gaining enhanced senses and dexterity, allowing them to perform a broader scope of manual tasks. This is likely to change the nature of work across industries and occupations." In response to their claim that 47% of current jobs will be replaced, Derek Thompson commented in *The Atlantic*, "It would be anxious enough if we knew exactly which jobs are next in line for automation. The truth is scarier. We don't really have a clue."[3]

As reported in the Scientific American, [4] "Our understanding of the relation between technological advances and employment is limited by outdated metrics. If productivity is no longer a good proxy for a vigorous economy, then we need a new way to measure economic health. In a 2009 report economists Joseph Stiglitz of Columbia University, Amartya Sen of Harvard University and Jean-Paul Fitoussi of the Paris Institute of Political Studies wrote that "the time is ripe for our measurement system to shift emphasis from measuring economic production to measuring people's well-being." (Report: bit.ly/1jPXSDx).

A 2014 report by Cornell's Industrial Relations School (IRL) called for statistical agencies to capture more and better data on job market churn—data that could help us learn which job losses stem from automation. "Without such data, we will never properly understand how technology is changing the nature of work in the 21st century—and what, if anything, should be done about it. As one participant in this year's roundtable put it, 'Even if this is just another industrial revolution, people underestimate how wrenching that is. If it is, what are the changes to the rules of labor markets and businesses that should be made this time? We made a lot last time. What is the elimination of child labor this time? What is the eight-hour workday this time?'"

In the Foreign Affairs article, "New World Order: Labor, Capital, and Ideas in the Power Law Economy" by Erik Brynjolfsson, Andrew McAfee, and Michael Spence, they write, "Should the digital revolution continue to be as powerful in the future as it has been in recent years, the structure of the modern economy and the role of work itself may need to be rethought. As a group, our descendants may work fewer hours and live better—but both the work and the rewards could be spread even more unequally, with a variety of unpleasant consequences. Creating sustainable, equitable, and inclusive growth will require more than business as usual. The place to start is with a proper understanding of just how fast and far things are evolving." [5]

Many analysts have come upon the idea that new technology can lead to higher unemployment and rising inequality. The British economist John Maynard Keynes coined the term "technological unemployment" back in the 1930s when he predicted the displacement of workers by machines. In the early 19th century, power looms introduced during the Industrial Revolution threatened to replace the artisans with less-skilled, low-wage laborers, leaving them without work. Enter the Luddites, the movement that set out to smash the power looms.

Great Read on the Post-Work Economy http://amzn.to/1plbbO2

Will we have 21st century Luddites using all their political power to smash the transformation of work, especially knowledge work that makes up the huge portion of the Services Economy? How will we distribute wealth in a Post-Work economy where technology tends to agriculture, industry and, now, services?

So, it's not just business transformation, it's societal transformation that we must now tend. Change won't come from the top, from the vested interests who want to cling to their economic and political power. It won't come from the bottom of organizations where folks are not fully informed and desperately cling to jobs with uncertain futures. It will be the middle of organizations, the places where innovation takes place, where new digital products and services are developed, where organizational restructuring occurs to adapt to the needed outside-in transformation demanded by today's fully informed customers. As business analysts and architects, our future is in your hands as you take on corporate social responsibility (CSR) and compliance, risk and governance issues (CRG).

You know, the term 'management' didn't exist until the Industrial Revolution demanded it and Fredrick Taylor, Alfred Sloan and Peter Drucker invented this thing we call management. From the early 20th century until today, it's been *command-and-control* management. In our current digital age, it must transform to *connect-and-collaborate*, where transparency becomes the invisible hand of management control. We cannot smash the smart machines that are taking over so much work in the services sectors with the Luddites' hammers. We can only chip away at the forms of governance that no longer work for the people by becoming fully informed citizens, fully informed workers.

According to the late James Martin, "The individual is immersed in such an expanding ocean of capability to process knowledge. That makes the twenty-first century both more exciting and more perilous than any other century so far. We are heading toward an inflection point, but our leaders are not preparing to make the passage smoother for us. That will be the job of the Transition Generation." According to Martin, today's young people will be the generation that brings about this great transition by understanding the 21st century roadmap and the critical role they will play in the massive change that is inevitable in this century.

The big problems facing the world today are not at all things beyond our control. Our biggest threat is not an asteroid about to crash into us, something we can do nothing about. Instead, all the major threats facing us today are problems entirely of our own making. And since we made the problems, we can also solve the problems. That then means that it's entirely in our power to deal with these problems. In particular, what can all of us do? For those of you who are interested in these choices, there are lots of things you can do. There's a lot that we don't understand, and that we need to understand. And there's a lot that we already do understand, but aren't doing, and that we need to be doing. — Jared Diamond, *Collapse: How Societies Choose to Fail or Succeed*? [6]

Here's Tom Davenport, reporting in the Wall Street Journal, "In short, I would conclude that in the field of high-end knowledge work, it's still unclear whether the ultimate fate of workers is to be replaced rather than to be augmented by technology. If there is any overall lesson, it is to make sure you are capable of augmenting an automated or semi-automated system. If the decisions and actions you make at work are remarkably similar to those made by a computer, that computer will probably be taking your paycheck before long. To prevent that, you must understand how these systems perform their jobs. You need to understand how they work, know their strengths and weaknesses, examine them regularly to make sure their decisions are good, and be able to document and improve them. It's probably not a bad idea to improve your human relationship skills, but you may also want to address your ability to have meaningful relationships with computers."
http://on.wsj.com/1ilMmn1

Geoff Livingston, author and president of Tenacity5 Media, wrote, "I see the movement towards AI and robotics as evolutionary, in large part because it is such a sociological leap. The technology may be ready, but we are not—at least, not yet."

Glenn Edens, a director of research in networking, security, and distributed systems within the Computer Science Laboratory at PARC, a Xerox Company, wrote, "There are significant technical and policy issues yet to resolve, however there is a relentless march on the part of commercial interests (businesses) to increase productivity so if the technical advances are reliable and have a positive ROI then there is a risk that workers will be displaced. Ultimately we need a broad and large base of employed population, otherwise there will be no one to pay for all of this new world."

Will networked, automated AI displace more jobs than it creates? That was precisely the question covered in "The 2014 Survey: Impacts of AI and robotics by 2025." It's a 67 page report that you'll want to review in order to frame your own thinking about the post-work society. Internet experts and highly engaged netizens participated in answering an eight-question survey fielded by Elon University and the Pew Internet Project. One of the survey questions asked respondents to share their answer to the following query:

"Self-driving cars, intelligent digital agents that can act for you, and robots are advancing rapidly. Will networked, automated, artificial intelligence (AI) applications and robotic devices have displaced more jobs than they have created by 2025? Describe your expectation about the degree to which robots, digital agents, and AI tools will have disrupted white collar and blue collar jobs by 2025 and the social consequences emerging from that."

Among the key themes emerging from 1,896 respondents' answers were: • Advances in technology may displace certain types of work, but historically they have been a net creator of jobs. • We will adapt to these changes by inventing entirely new types of work, and by taking advantage of uniquely human capabilities. • Technology will free us from day-to-day drudgery, and allow us to define our relationship with "work" in a more positive and socially beneficial way. • Ultimately, we as a society control our own destiny through the choices we make. • Automation has thus far impacted mostly blue-collar employment; the coming wave of innovation threatens to upend white-collar work as well. • Certain highly-skilled workers will succeed wildly in this new environment—but far more may be displaced into lower-paying service industry jobs at best, or permanent unemployment at worst. • Our educational system is not adequately preparing us for work of the future, and our political and economic institutions are not prepared to handle this future.

AI, Robotics, and the Future of Jobs

Experts envision automation and intelligent digital agents permeating vast areas of our work and personal lives by 2025, but they are divided on whether advances will displace more jobs than they create. Some say the education system and political and economic institutions are not well prepared for this revolution.

http://bit.ly/1pW22uU

So, the question is, "What are people for in a world that does not need their labor, and where only a minority are needed to guide the 'bot-based economy?" How will we organize our world if machines can provide goods and services at lower and lower costs while fewer and fewer have income enough to buy anything? As Stow Boyd puts it, "The end state is uncertain, but we are headed toward a disruption of our society on the same order of magnitude as the rise of agriculture and industrialism, but in a much more compressed time frame: decades, not generations or centuries. And that question—what are people for?—will taunt us because it's unclear if there is an answer or whether it is just an irresolvable dilemma." [7] Get informed:

Stanford economist Russ Roberts, for one, knew Adam Smith's *The Wealth of Nations* inside and out, but *Moral Sentiments* sat on his shelf for nearly 30 years until he finally picked it up and gave it a read. Now, Roberts calls the book a "marvel" and a "road map to happiness, goodness, and self-knowledge" that completely changed his life. "Even though he's the father of capitalism and wrote the most famous and maybe the best book ever on why some nations are rich and others are poor," Roberts, host of the popular podcast EconTalk, writes in his new book, *How Adam Smith Can Change Your Life*, "Adam Smith in *The Theory of Moral Sentiments* wrote as eloquently as anyone ever has on the futility of pursuing money with the hope of finding happiness."

At first glance, there may seem to be inconsistency between Smith's two works—one that advocates economic self-interest, and the other that suggests empathy and altruism are as natural to us as eating and sleeping. But for Smith, these two points are not as discordant as they might seem. Smith suggests in *The Theory of Moral Sentiments* that both the individual and society benefit if we pursue our own interest through virtuous actions.

THE APOCALYPSE

"Now this is not the end. It is not even the beginning of the end. But it is, perhaps, the end of the beginning."—Winston Churchill

The Mayan Apocalypse of December 21, 2012 was not the end-of-the-world as we know it, but in Greek apocalypse means the "lifting of the veil." It is a disclosure of something hidden from the majority of mankind in an era dominated by falsehood and misconception. Mayan elders did not prophesy that everything will come to an end. Rather, this is a time of transition from one World Age into another. The Mayan fifth world finished in 1987. The sixth world started in 2012, placing us at the beginning of a new age. It is the time for humans to work through "our stuff" individually and collectively. The Mayan sixth world is nothing more than a blank slate; it is up to us to create the new world and civilization as we wish.

Although it is impossible to know precisely how cognitive computing will change our lives, a likely possibility is that there are two overall potential outcomes. 1) Mankind will be set free from the drudgery of work, or 2) we will see the end of the human era.

1) *Extreme Optimism and Techno-utopianism.* *"The automation of work across every sector of the market economy is already beginning to free up human labor to migrate to the evolving social economy. If the steam engine freed human beings from feudal bondage to pursue material self-interest in the capitalist marketplace, the Internet of Things frees human beings from the market economy to pursue nonmaterial shared interests. Intelligent technology will do most of the heavy lifting in an economy centered on abundance rather than scarcity. A half century from now, our grandchildren are likely to look back at the era of mass employment in the market with the same sense of utter disbelief as we look upon slavery and serfdom in former times."* — Jeremy Rifkin, *The Zero Marginal Cost Society*.

2) *Extreme Pessimism.* *"In support of achieving their goals, Artificial Super Intelligence (ASI) machines may compete with humans for valuable resources in a way that jeopardizes human life. ASI machines will replicate themselves quickly*

and independently. Combined with nanotechnology, "thinking" machines could very quickly "eat up the environment". —James Barrat, *Our Final Invention: Artificial Intelligence and the End of the Human Era.*

With technology racing forward at an exponential rate, tending to our agriculture, industries, and services, it is time for us to act now individually and collectively to land somewhere in between extreme 1) and 2). The veil to the cognitive computing economy and society has already been lifted.

We must evolve a fundamentally new economics, one based not on the 20th century reality of scarcity but on a new 21st century reality of abundance that can be shared equitably between capital and labor.

Then considering how our current 20th century educational system, curriculums and school rooms are based on standardization of tasks to be performed, even more interesting, according to Robinson, "We need to unlearn the habit of acting like machines and relearn how to act like humans." Quite likely this means, as Robinson has been pointing out in his amazing TED talks, going back to what we did as children: playfulness, experimentation, listening, imagining, dreaming and failing fast, failing cheap and trying again. Paradoxically, maybe having smart machines gathering data, information and to some extent knowledge, may actually free us up to do just that and focus on nurturing creativity and attaining wisdom. Watch: bit.ly/MLwKdt Also see "Can we make learning as much fun as video games?" tinyurl.com/nbxxhwj

Larry Summers, a former American treasury secretary, observed employment trends among American men between 25 and 54. In the 1960s only one in 20 of those men was not working. According to Mr. Summers' extrapolations, in ten years the number could be one in seven. [8]

The Machine Intelligence Research Institute (MIRI) is a non-profit organization founded in 2000 to research safety issues related to the development of Strong AI. The organization advocates ideas initially put forth by I. J. Good and Vernor Vinge regarding an "intelligence explosion", or Singularity, which MIRI thinks may follow the creation of sufficiently advanced AI. Research fellow Eliezer Yudkowsky coined the term "Friendly AI" to refer to a hypothetical super-intelligent AI that has a positive impact on humanity. The organization has argued that to be "Friendly" a self-improving AI needs to be constructed in a transparent, robust, and stable way. MIRI was formerly known as the Singularity Institute, and before that as the Singularity Institute for Artificial Intelligence. http://intelligence.org/

The Future of Humanity Institute (FHI) is an interdisciplinary research centre focused on predicting and preventing large-scale risks to human civilization. It was founded in 2005 as part of the Faculty of Philosophy and the Oxford Martin School at the University of Oxford, England. Its director is philosopher Nick Bostrom, and its research staff and associates include futurist Anders Sandberg, engineer K. Eric Drexler, economist Robin Hanson, and Giving What We Can founder Toby Ord. http://www.fhi.ox.ac.uk

An existential risk is one that threatens the existence of our entire species. The Cambridge Centre for the Study of Existential Risk (CSER) — a joint initiative between a philosopher, a scientist, and a software entrepreneur — was founded on the conviction that these risks require a great deal more scientific investigation than they presently receive. CSER is a multidisciplinary research centre dedicated to the study and mitigation of risks that could lead to human extinction. Its goal is to steer a small fraction of Cambridge's great intellectual resources, and of the reputation built on its past and present scientific pre-eminence, to the task of ensuring that our own species has a long-term future. Its advisors include no less than Stephen Hawking.

CENTRE FOR THE STUDY OF EXISTENTIAL RISK
UNIVERSITY OF CAMBRIDGE

http://cser.org/

POLICY MAKERS - GOOD LUCK WITH THEM

Policy makers and societies need to prepare for future technology, too. To do this well, they will need a clear understanding of how technology might shape the global economy and society over the coming decade. They will need to decide how to invest in new forms of education and infrastructure, and figure out how disruptive economic change will affect comparative advantages. Governments will need to create an environment in which citizens can continue to prosper, even as emerging technologies disrupt their lives.

In September 2014, a Harvard Business School study titled "*An Economy Doing Half its Job*," said American companies, particularly big ones, were showing some signs of recovering their competitive edge on the world stage since the financial crisis, but that workers would likely keep struggling to demand better pay and benefits.

"We argue that such a divergence is unsustainable," according to the report, which was based on a survey of 1,947 of Harvard Business School alumni around the globe, and which highlighted problems with the U.S. education system, transport infrastructure, and the ineffectiveness of the political system." Many federal officials appear more concerned with making partisan gains than improving America's economy. As a result, the federal government seems at times to be the biggest impediment to U.S. competitiveness." [9] (Link to the full report: http://tinyurl.com/mm6ea4s).

Duh. Who hasn't argued for transformation in the U.S. education system, transport infrastructure, and the ineffectiveness of the political system? But as the Princeton university study reveals, the U.S. is no longer a democracy; it is now an oligarchy (some call it a plutonomy, whilst the rest of the population, is a *precariat*). To break the government of the corporation, by the corporation and for the corporation, the pain levels in society may reach such acute levels that the French Revolution 2.0 may indeed happen.

Billionaire, Nick Hanauer wrote an article, "The Pitchforks Are Coming... For Us Plutocrats." In his memo to fellow zillionaires he wrote, "The most ironic thing about rising inequality is how completely unnecessary and self-defeating it is. If we do something about it, if we adjust our policies in the way that, say, Franklin D. Roosevelt did during the Great Depression—so that we help the 99 percent and preempt the revolutionaries and crazies, the ones with the pitchforks—that will be the best thing possible for us rich folks, too. It's not just that we'll escape with our lives; it's that we'll most certainly get even richer.

"The model for us rich guys here should be Henry Ford, who realized that all his autoworkers in Michigan weren't only cheap labor to be exploited; they were consumers, too. Ford figured that if he raised their wages, to a then-exorbitant $5 a day, they'd be able to afford his Model Ts. What a great idea. My suggestion to you is: Let's do it all over again. We've got to try something. These idiotic trickle-down policies are destroying my customer base. And yours too." [10] (Read the full article: http://tinyurl.com/lo5t6f6).

IDEAS FOR CHANGE

Although this brief book has been all about a wakeup call, and an early-warning report, I now want to put forward what we might be doing as individuals, as companies, as governments and society as a whole.

Overall. These are not my proprietary ideas but the ideas of thought leaders from around the globe. Rebuilding a broad global middle class will be difficult. One thing is clear, however. We won't be able to revive shared prosperity without strengthening the voice of workers at the workplace and in our politics. What was once scorned as an archaic leftover of an old economy is now clearly a vital ingredient to reviving democracy – and the so-called American dream. Following are some of the ideas for change floating around the Web.

- Guaranteed Income, Guaranteed Jobs. "Love and work are the cornerstones of our humanness."— Sigmund Freud. Thus any guaranteed income must account for "work." Work produces self-worth via mastery, and purpose and although the work won't necessarily be of the current wage labor variety, all forms of work can eliminate idleness and boredom (the Devil's Workshop). Laissez-faire economist Milton Friedman proposed a Negative Income Tax (NIT) in the 1960s to address the problems of the poor. A negative income tax is intended to create a single system that would not only pay for government, but would also fulfill the social goal of making sure that there was a minimum level of income for all.
- Direct hire programs that create a School Improvement Corps, a Park Improvement Corps, and a Student Jobs Corps, among others.
- Public Works Programs. The New Deal 2.0 would involve setting up a massive public works program to provide full employment and address the needs of society. There are plenty of important projects: building high quality public transportation systems, developing solar power, rebuilding the infrastructure, creating new industries, and building new schools and community centers. Workers would be retrained as necessary to become part of these new industries. Public works programs are not new. Most roads, bridges, railroads, and dams were built through public works pro-

grams that provided millions of jobs, e.g., the New Deal's "3 Rs:" Relief, Recovery, and Reform. That is Relief for the unemployed and poor; Recovery of the economy to normal levels; and Reform of the financial system.

- A 30-Hour Workweek with No Loss of Pay or Benefits. An immediate step to achieve full employment would be to reduce the workweek to 30 hours, with no loss in pay or benefits. This would distribute all the existing work between the employed and unemployed. This stops one section of the working class from being thrown out of work and becoming destitute.
- Taxation Shift from Labor to Capital. With the bulk of prosperity going to capital versus labor, it would seem that taxes on capital should be higher than that on labor. The higher the level of public expenditure and the income elasticity of labor supply, the less should capital income be subsidized and the more it should be taxed. Not taxing capital implies that labor must be taxed at a higher rate. Taxing capital at lower rates than labor can lead to increased inequality; while equality of outcomes is not desirable in a capitalist system, excessive inequality can cause problems as well. And, let's face it, we are in the Gilded Age 2.0. Oliver Wendell Holmes once said, "I like to pay taxes. With them I buy civilization." Roughly 30 percent of the burden of U.S. corporate income taxes is borne by U.S. capital; 70 percent by labor. In the current age of inequality, something is wrong with this picture, especially in light of capital tax loopholes and tax inversion by multinational corporations.
- A Progressive Transaction Tax. Under a transaction tax, every individual, rich or poor, and every company, big or small, would pay the same flat tax on transactions. With everybody paying their equal share, we would all benefit from much lower tax burdens, more money in our pockets and a growing economy. Other taxing models include the Value Added Tax (VAT).
- Peer Economy. Use Uber to catch a ride, or run chores through Amazon's Mechanical Turk or TaskRabbit, rent a room at an Airbnb, or sell crafts on Etsy or rent on street parking with Monkey, or rent office space from LooseCubes, and you are disrupting the traditional hierarchical organization. But not so fast. The P2P economy (sharing economy) represents only a tiny fraction of the millions of people out of work. But, then again, it could grow to be substantial not only for those who currently participate, but for those yet to be displaced by artificial intelligence.

- United Nations Commission on Post Industrial Work. Maybe H.G Wells' 1920s writings on One World State versus today's many nation states could serve as a baseline. With globalization in full tilt, why are there 196 nation states?

Business. As a business, how you change is going to be dramatic and transformational, or else you won't be a business in the near future.

TechCast Global is a research-based corporation that grew out of George Washington University. The experts examine the technology revolution, globalization, and other transformative changes that are driving the creative destruction of markets, introducing disruptive products and services, and altering the way organizations work—yet today's managers lack useful knowledge on how to plan for these critical challenges. Techcast's authoritative, comprehensive forecasts help managers and planners adapt to this rapidly changing world.

Here is what some of the experts suggest for change:

- Ensure [somehow] "friendly" Super Intelligent machines
- Switch from growth econometrics to Sustainability to reverse/fix the rapid degradation of the ecosystem
- Population right sized to what, at a given tech level, the ecosystem can support to address life extension and the finite sized ecosystem
- Renewable Energy including halophytes, salt plants grown on wastelands
- Comfortable guaranteed middle class income for everyone, machines owned by the global commons/ produce the wealth to provide the requisite income to address the machines taking the jobs
- Reduced requirement for physical infrastructures enabled by Tele-everything, tele-travel, tele-shopping, distributed energy generation, global brain, global sensor grid, and the cloud

> ✓ To keep an eye on the future of business, stop by
> www.techcastglobal.com
> and MIT Sloan's Center for Digital Business (IDE): mitsloan.mit.edu/ide
> Download the presentations at: http://bit.ly/ZVHr4O
> Join the Cognitive Systems Institute's Linkedin group:
> http://tinyurl.com/lfk3aqr
> Check out the latest at the Singularity University: http://singularityu.org and http://singularityhub.com
> Check out: http://syntheticneurobiology.org
> And if your specific interest is information technology (IT) check out the Global Institute for IT Management: www.globaliim.com

Here are some of my specific suggestions for businesses:

- Get informed and stay informed by participating in the standards groups for your industry (e.g., the Industrial Internet Consortium).
- Form a team to track the expanding literature on Cognitive Computing as there's a lot coming down the pike. It's also a good idea to set a Web search "alert:" "artificial intelligence" + "your industry." Add the Cognitive Computing component to your BPM Center of Excellence (CoE) or your R&D

department.

- No matter where you are on the process maturity curve, pounce on your IT and BPM service providers and build strategies with them, for this stuff will be done. Traditional booksellers and retailers shied away from that once scary technology, the Internet —until they got Amazoned! Don't get blindsided by a new competitor from nowhere who "gets it" today.
- Reach out to universities that have begun offering Cognitive Computing courses, e.g., Carnegie Mellon University, New York University (NYU), The Ohio State University, Rensselaer Polytechnic Institute (RPI), University of California, Berkeley, University of Michigan and the University of Texas in Austin.
- Reach out to the relevant Cognitive Computing startups, several that are mentioned in this book. Experiment with their offerings to stay on top of new ways you can use technology to make your high-impact performers even better and to raise the performance of (or cut the costs associated with) lower-impact people.
- According to innovation designer and futurist Vito Di Bari in 2014, "The entire world will change in such a way that people with a technological background (notably today's CIOs and CTOs) will be the ones who will be asked to lead the companies of the future towards success." http://bit.ly/1EFbu0d   I coauthored such ideas in a CIO magazine article way back in 2005 pointing to the same conclusion. http://bit.ly/1oZeZ7L Now, more than ever, the time has come.
- Remember one thing, "The only sustainable competitive advantage is an organization's ability to learn faster than the competition." — Peter Senge, *The Fifth Discipline*
- Keep up at CognitiveTrends.com

---

[1] http://tinyurl.com/mwag29b
[2] http://bit.ly/1mj2qSJ
[3] http://theatln.tc/1dRHDqd
[4] http://tinyurl.com/jwrwftw
[5] http://tinyurl.com/lbdlq2k
[6] http://tinyurl.com/orlwqqu
[7] http://tinyurl.com/jwrwftw
[8] http://tinyurl.com/lbf3zfp
[9] http://tinyurl.com/mm6ea4s
[10] http://tinyurl.com/lo5t6f6

CPSIA information can be obtained
at www.ICGtesting.com
Printed in the USA
BVOW11s2241150816
459093BV00001B/1/P

9 780929 652511